First published in Great Britain in 2002

400 YEARS IN TORCROSS

1602–2002
A Pictorial History

Copyright © Robin Rose-Price
ISBN 1 898964 52 1

Published by Orchard Publications
2 Orchard Close, Chudleigh, Devon TQ13 0LR
Telephone 01626 852714

Printed by
Hedgerow Print
Crediton EX17 1ES

Contents

Acknowledgements

When Bob Roberts (who sadly died two years ago) was researching his local histories of the area, he came up with a date for the first habitation of Torcross, 1602. His research is displayed in this book and 2002 seemed a good opportunity to celebrate Torcross's 400th birthday.

The wealth of photographs and memories prompted an exhibition, which somehow took on life of its own. Opening in March 2002, in Torcross Chapel, it ran for twenty one days. Such was the enthusiasm in the village that there was no problem finding six stewards a day to man the exhibition. It was visited by 2,700 people, and £1100 was raised for the chapel after expenses. Having assembled all the material and interest being so great it seemed a tragedy to let it all dissipate again so a publisher was approached to see if a book could be produced and so make this collection available to all.

For a small village clinging onto the margins, Torcross has had an exciting and varied history. As problems of climate and position and politics were resolved, it has evolved into the twenty first century. Many interesting books have been published and it is from their superior research that we have compiled the captions and understood some of Torcross's evolution. These books include Grace Bradbeer's *The Land that Changed its Face* the story of the evacuation of 1942, Bob Roberts' pamphlets, Robin Stanes' first book published in 1983 *Slapton – a Fortunate Place*, Arthur L. Clamp's *Exercises Tiger and Fabius*, Harold Fox's *Evolution of the Fishing Villages* and Ray Freeman of the Dartmouth History Research Group's *D-Day Remembered*. Thanks also to the Dartmouth Museum for permission to use some of their archive photographs of the U.S. Forces and to Devon County Council for permission to use the water colours by William Payne.

Many local people in the village should also be mentioned for their contributions and encouragement and we would like to thank Bill and May Sanders, Ray and Anne Pengelly, the Venmore family, John and Kathleen Hannaford, Una and Ray Taster, Bill and Jane Ireland, Susan Rendle, Howard Garner, Angie Lansdale, Ken Small, Jean Edwards, Brian Stone, Joan Breach, the Wheldon family, Pat May, Ralph Blank, Mary Rogers and Brian Smalley. Special thanks also to the Dartmouth Museum and the Cookworthy Musuem in Kingsbridge who lent us photographs and memorabilia. Ian Davidson kindly gave us permission to use Ted Archer's 'Excercise Tiger' painting. Pat Nettleton helped with the publicity for the exhibition, and Reg Hannaford, blessed with a fine interest in the village, narrative skills, humour and a great memory, was a fund of information.

Lastly, I must mention mention Robin Rose-Price (and his long-suffering wife Alison), without whose energy and hard work there would have been no exhibition and no book. It has been a pleasure working with him.

We hope the residents of Torcross and the many friends the village has, will continue to cherish memories of village life, so that in another 400 years there will be many different memories, inconceivable to us today!

Clare Pawley

This map shows Henry VIII's fortifications for our part of the coast.

The defence of the sands was a problem in Tudor times and was only considered safe after the Armada and many of the marauding pirate ships were vanquished. It appears that the Ley acted as a moat to defend Slapton, and had a drawbridge, where the present bridge now stands.

The map shows Slapton Sands fortified each end with a castle. The castle shown at Slapton Bridge says 'not made' at the side, although other castles on the plan 'not made' were built, including Fort Charles and Dartmouth Castle. 'It may well be, in fact, that the two castles shown on the chart at what must be Torcross and Strete Gate, could at one time train their guns along the vulnerable Long Sands'.
(from Slapton – a Fortunate Place by Robin Stanes).

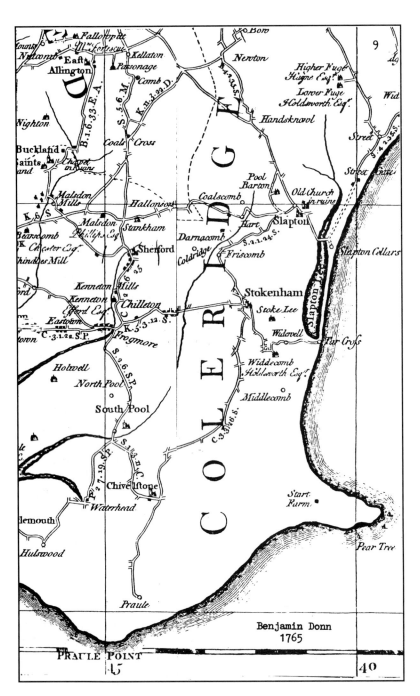

1765 Map of Coleridge Hundred by Benjamin Donn

The county of Devon was divided into 33 districts known as 'hundreds'.
They are listed below:–

1. Axminster	12. South Molton	23. Woodford
2. Culliton	13. Sherwell	24. Lifton
3. East Budley	14. Branton	25. Tavestock
4. St Mary Ottery	15. Fremington	26. Roborough
5. Clifton	16. North Tawton	27. Plimpton
6. Hayrudge	17. Winckley	28. Armington
7. Haymock	18. Shebbeare	29. Stanborough
8. Halberton	19. Hartland	30. Colridge
9. Tiverton	20. Black Torrington	31. Heytor
10. Bampton	21. Crediton	32. Tinbridge
11. Witheridge	22. Weft Budley	33. Exminster

Foot note:– A 'Hundred' was a division having its own court.
Farms were given as great a prominence as the villages.

Manorial record of 29th March 1602

Stokenham

Beeson

Widicombe

Widewell

Kernborough

Kernborough

South Allington

Coleridge

Chillington

Frittiscombe

Torcross

Start

THE BIRTH OF TORCROSS *Original research by Bob Roberts.*

One hundred years after the Norman Conquest, Stokenham became a manor. Thereafter, for 500 years, it was firmly ruled by a succession of feudal lords whose base was the manor house at Stokenham, east of the church. (The manor house fell into ruins around 1600 and is represented now only by irregular mounds scattered over the surface of the fields next to the church on the seaward side).

The administrative instrument by which these powerful lords ruled the manor was the manorial court held every few weeks in the great hall of the manor house at Stokenham. Every village or settlement in the manor – and there were about twenty of them from 1300 onwards – had to send its representatives to these regular courts. The representatives reported on events in their communities: the steward presiding over the court and representing the lord then dispensed any necessary instructions, judgements or punishments.

For centuries, Torcross was never represented at these manorial courts, because nobody lived at Torcross. There had been fishermen working from the Torcross beaches for a thousand years. They had their fish-houses, their drying grounds and their workshops on or near the beach, but they lived inland – particularly at Widewell, because for centuries there had been the threat of pirates raiding, pillaging and robbing along the coastline.

In Tudor times that began to change. By the time of Queen Elizabeth the great English mariners such as Drake had begun to make England a sea power. The pirate raids diminished and disappeared. The fishermen began to take their families down to the coast to live, close by their work. A community began to come into being, living at Torcross.

The existence of that new community was officially recognised for the first time on Monday 29th March in the year 1602, being the forty fourth year of the reign of Queen Elizabeth. On that memorable day, Torcross for the first time, as a newly-born community took its place among all the other settlements of Stokenham and made its presentation formally at the manorial court. The attached document records the events, being a facsimile of the parchment roll recording the events of the manorial court on that day.

The heading of the court record read, when translated from the Latin:
The court of the manor of Stokenham held there on the 29th day of March in the 44th year of the reign of our lady the Queen Elizabeth.

Down the left hand side are the names of the various settlements Beeson, Dunstone, Wydecombe, Wydewill, East Kernborough and so on, followed in each instance by the report of the settlement.

Right at the bottom of the list is the new entry, appearing for the very first time, **Torcrosse**. The report then says: 'The tenants of this place, being sworn, came and reported that all was well'. Thereafter, Torcross appears at every court: the new settlement has been born.

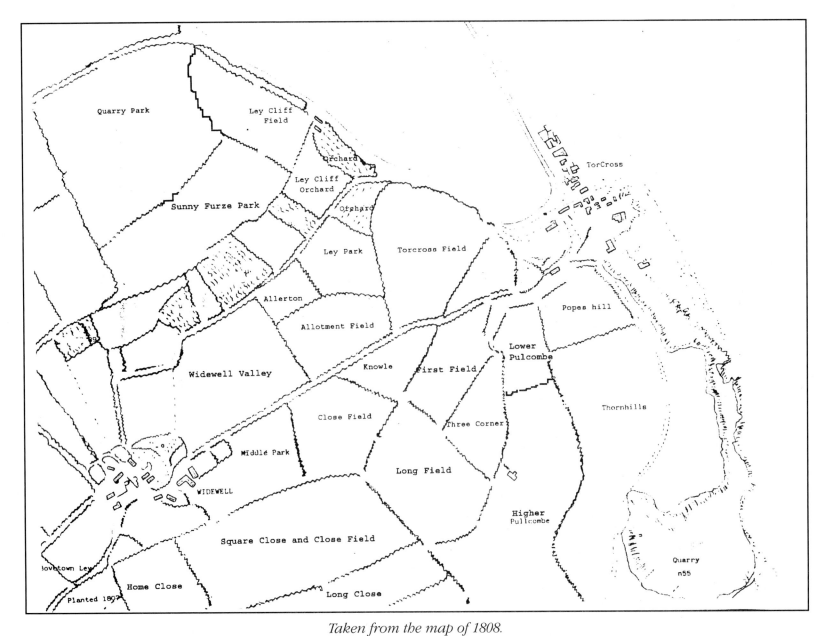

Taken from the map of 1808.
The boundaries and names have changed in a few instances, but the local farmers still use the ancient field names when discussing crop and livestock rotation.

How did Torcross get its name?

1. **Tor**   being an outcrop of rock.
   Cross   being a stone cross.

Legend has it that long ago there was a cross on the rocky peninsula at the southern end of the village. 'A cross in this location would have been used as a navigation aid and also for devotional purposes for those whose livelihoods depended on God's command over the sea'. (Harold Fox: *Evolution of the fishing villages*)

The story says that the cross was removed by the lord of Widdicombe Manor and placed in his own grounds, where it still stands today.

2. **Tar**   as in bitumen
   Crofs   as in small dwellings

Old maps refer to Tar Crofs. At that time the fishermen and their families started to live on the coast. They dipped their nets and ropes into boiling tar to preserve and waterproof them.

3. *Torcross could also have been names after two prominent families in the area at that time. 1281 Walter de la Torre and 1316 Adam de la Cros.

* From H.J. Yallop's booklet on *Start Bay*

1944 photo of cross by Widdicombe House

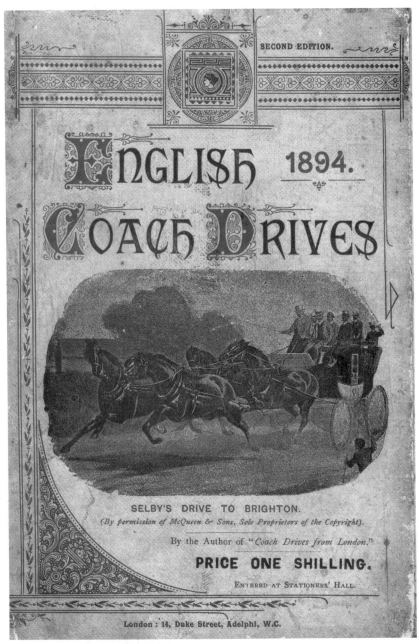

Front cover of English Coach Drives booklet, 1894.

DARTMOUTH AND KINGSBRIDGE.

THE "PIONEER" and "VIVID" Coaches leave DARTMOUTH for KINGSBRIDGE, *viâ* TORCROSS,* DAILY (Sundays excepted) as follows :—

				"VIVID."		"PIONEER."
Dartmouth	...	...	*depart*	9.30 a.m.	...	1.10 p.m.
Kingsbridge	...	...	*arrive*	1.40 p.m.	...	4.30 ,,
,,	...	...	*depart*	1.50 ,,	...	4.55 ,,
Dartmouth	...	...	*arrive*	5. 5 ,,	...	8.10 ,,

* *Change horses.*

FARES.

				Single.		Return.
Dartmouth and Torcross	...	...	...	**2s.**	...	**3s.**
,, ,, Kingsbridge	...	...	...	**3s. 6d.**	...	**5s. 6d.**
Torcross ,, ,,	...	...	...	**1s. 6d.**	...	**2s. 6d.**

Proprietors—THE DARTMOUTH COACHING COMPANY, LIMITED.

Manager—Mr. W. VICKERY, "Torcross Hotel," near Kingsbridge.

THE history of the above coaches dates back to the year 1873, and the opening scene was laid at the "Sands Hotel," Slapton, the principal actor being Mr. W. Vickery. This gentleman had taken the "Sands Hotel," situated about half way between Dartmouth and Kingsbridge, in 1872; he soon discovered that he could not get his daily papers the same day as they were published, and wishing to keep himself informed of what was going on in the world in general, and our tight little island in particular, he conceived the decidedly enterprising idea of running a coach on his own account *to fetch his own private letters and daily papers*, trusting to luck, no doubt, that the coach would soon get known to the travelling public, and fill up. Needless to say, he found it a very losing game at first, and, to use his own words, "he

43

worked it three years at a great loss, especially the first year." However, Mr. Vickery was plucky enough to try it a fourth year, with the satisfactory result that he found it beginning to pay ; so he secured a partner in the person of Mr. Tucker, of Kingsbridge, and together they kept the coach going (and paying) till 1884, when the demand for seats had become so great that they started a second coach, and ran both all the year round until 1887. In 1888 Mr. Tucker retired from the enterprise, and Mr. Vickery worked both coaches on his own account for the next three years, when he turned it into the present company—but retaining the management himself— and so popular had the road become that a third coach, the "Comet," was at once put on from Torrcross to Dartmouth and back (via Kingsbridge), and has been running daily, summer and winter, ever since.

Before giving a description of the road traversed, let me assure nervous passengers that they have coachmen with records :—E. Sanders, the coachman of the "Pioneer," has been with Mr. Vickery twenty-one and a-half years, has driven 201,880 miles, and carried 110,639 passengers in that time without an accident.

J. Distin, coachman of the "Comet," first served Mr. Vickery ten and a-half years ago, and during that period has driven 100,940 miles, and carried 57,113 passengers for his master, without an accident.

S. Evans, coachman of the "Vivid," although he has only been six months or so in his present place, has driven 2808 miles, and carried 992 passengers, also without accident.

Leaving Dartmouth by the Newcomen Road, we pass Dartmouth **Old Castle** on the left, and soon arrive at **War-fleet** ; the steep ascent in front of us is **Week Hill,** from the summit of which, some 500 feet above sea level, we get a capital view of Dartmouth Harbour behind us, whilst in front is **Start Bay,** with **Start Point** and its lighthouse beyond.

Half a mile further on we enter the pretty little village of **Stokefleming,** the first house of which, on the left, Stoke Lodge, was the property of the late George Bidder, C.E. Leaving Stokefleming behind us, we descend the somewhat lengthy **Blackpool Hill,** and get a view of **Blackpool Bay,** to which there is a right-of-way through a pretty "drive," much patronised by pic-nic and other parties in summer time. Having arrived at the bottom of Blackpool Hill, we have an equally long and somewhat steeper hill—to wit, **Strete Hill**— to climb, on the summit of which is the quaint little village of **Strete.** Our next mile of road, down to the Slapton Sands, commands a capital view of the country in front of us, including **Slapton Lea** and **Torrcross** (two inland freshwater lakes, teeming with fish and wild fowl), **Busands, Hallsands,** &c. The Lea is only separated from the sea by the beach and a narrow strip of land, along which we shall presently drive, and reminds one very much of the Earl of Ilchester's famous swanery at Abbotsbury, Dorsetshire. For the next two and a-half miles our road lies between the sea and Slapton Lea to Torrcross, where we pull up at the "Torrcross Hotel." Whilst a fresh team of horses are being "put to," passengers have ample time to sample the good things in host Vickery's hospitable hostelry.

Having again taken our seats on the coach, we leave Torrcross behind, and soon pass **Stokeley House** and grounds, the property of Sir R. Newman, Bart., and a little further on notice the fine old church of Stokenham on our right, the pretty vicarage grounds being on our left. The next point of interest is the straggling village of **Chillington,** after leaving which the long-since disused **Winslade Slate Quarry** is seen on our left, and we then come to **Frogmore** village, some three miles from Kingsbridge. An arm of the Kingsbridge and Salt-combe estuary runs up to this village, and small vessels at times discharge their cargoes here. Half a mile from Frogmore is **East Charleton**, and about three-quarters of a mile further we come to **West Charleton**, the most notable feature of which is its fine old church, on the tower of which still remains to be seen the old arch at one time forming a shelter for the Curfew bell. Crossing an arm of the Kingsbridge Estuary by means of a stone bridge, we rattle past the cemetery and a small shipbuilding yard on to the quay, and reach the town of Kingsbridge, and our journey's end.

N.B.—When visiting London do not fail to book seats for Theatres, Concerts, Music Halls, etc., at Keith Prowse & Co.'s various Box Offices in " Métropole," " Grand," " Victoria," " Savoy," " Langham," and other Hotels—48, Cheapside, etc. Seats in best positions always on hand."

Edward Sanders, coachman of the Pioneer, 1873–1900.

The Coach picked up passengers from Dartmouth Station, which was the only operating British Rail station in the country with no rail track running to it. Photo 1924. End of an era – the last coach leaves Dartmouth driven by Lewis Guest

Circa 1893. Passing through the narrow main road in the centre of Stoke Fleming.

Before 1856 the road from Dartmouth to Stoke Fleming was a turnpike, meaning that tolls were paid to use them.

The road between Stoke Fleming and Strete gate was a parish road, and had to be maintained by each parish it passed through. This was paid for by contributions from the parishioners.

Once the tunnel had been built at Torcross, to enable a reliable road to be laid along Slapton Sands, the whole road became a turnpike with each parish collecting its own tolls. This is why there are so many 'Turnpike Cottages' along the route.

A long pull up the hill above Blackpool Sands.

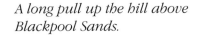

The last house in Strete still has the name Turnpike Cottage.

1850s view down the original coast road, now part of the South West coast path, descending to Strete Gate. (From a painting by W. Payne).

1912. Passengers were dropped off at the Royal Sands Hotel while they took Sportsmans' or Bathing Holidays.

The coaches passed the houses on beach-side road on Torcross sea front.

The horses were changed at the stable at the Torcross Hotel. Four horses were needed for the steep hills between Torcross and Dartmouth, but only three were needed for the journey to Kingsbridge.

The unsealed road out of Torcross by 'Lane End'.

The only road through Stokenham wound its way between the Inn and St Michael and All Angels Church. The thatched barn in the foreground stood where the car park now is.

Stokenham Church.

14

1898. The road outside the Tradesman's Arms has changed little in the last 100 years.

1890. A peaceful section of the road through Chillington, between Tanpits Lane and the old dairy.

1885. The road alongside Charleton Court Farm and the field where the Village Hall now stands.

1894. New bridge across Bowcombe Creek, showing the swing bridge that allowed barges to deliver limestone to the kilns for burning. The powdered stone was then spread on the land to adjust the acidity. The bearings used in the swing bridge were old canon balls.

1890. Embankment Road, Kingsbridge, showing the bonded warehouses where the Crabshell Inn now stands. A building supplier now occupies the field in the foreground

1909. New passengers have boarded the coach for the return trip to Dartmouth. Kingsbridge Station is now occupied by the industrial estate above a supermarket.

The changing face of transport in Torcross

1912. Gradually the horse drawn vehicles gave way to the motor car. The first cars to appear in Torcross belonged to the wealthy second home owners who had helped change Torcross from a peaceful fishing village into a popular seaside resort.

It may be interesting to note that a railway line was proposed in 1899 which would have gone through Slapton and Torcross and down the valley to Frogmore, Kingsbridge and Modbury. It was felt that Slapton Sands would be a good place for an experimental electric railway. Although there was support for this the Newman family objected and the project was shelved.

Information from Robin Stanes *Slapton – a Fortunate Place*, 1983

1914–1918. First World War.
The 5th Devonshire Regiment on cycle patrol. A big difference to the mechanisation brought to the village for Exercise Tiger in 1944.

Perhaps the bicycles had replaced the cavalry horses!

One of the first cars to arrive in Torcross in 1902. The dress code of the driver was typical of this period.

Cars became bigger and more numerous as the owners became aware that their car was a symbol of their standing in the world.

People began to use their cars for everyday use such as shopping and trips to the seaside.

Exuberant young people in holiday mood is not a new occurrence. This photo was taken in 1910 showing Ken Crisford demonstrating how many friends could be carried in this car.

They are being watched by Annie and George Crisford outside Hannaford's butchers shop.

1928. Mass tourism arrives in Torcross and relatively cheap trips along the coast were available in open charabancs. This meant that for the first time the 'less well off' could enjoy some of the pleasures previously only accessible to the rich.

1928. The Crowing Cock tea-rooms and restaurant began to flourish with the increase in numbers of visitors.

1908. Alfred, son of coach driver Lewis Guest, started up a delivery round with one of the first motorised delivery vans. Tragically he was killed in the trenches of the First World War.

1920s. Not everyone could afford a car and for some it was still a pleasure to collect the groceries from the village store by pony and trap.

Not everybody welcomed change.

Mr Baker from Stokeley Farm continued to deliver his milk in a churn from the back of his pony and trap into the late 1930s .

After a lifetime of driving horse drawn carriages for 'The Dartmouth Coaching Company', Lewis Guest continued as a carrier until his retirement. He would meet the train at Kingsbridge Station and collect any parcels etc. Then he would go up Fore Street to the various shops such as 'Tanners' to pick up any orders for delivery along his route through Charleton, Frogmore, Chillington, Stokenham and Torcross.

Lewis Guest was popular with all the children along his route. In exchange for a lift on the roof of his cart, the children used to deliver the parcels to the doors of the houses in their own village before Lewis moved onto the next destination.

Delivery to Widdicombe House above Torcross with four Torcross lads on the roof (from right to left) Mike Sutton, Bill Sanders, George Hannaford and Reg Hannaford.

Start Bay Slate Quarry

Beesands Cellars and road to the quarry.

1930s footpath from Torcross to the quarry along the bottom of Thornhills Field and down Jacob's Ladder.

The slate quarry appears on maps from 1747 but by 1885 was described as 'disused'.

The posters advertise the sale of the lease by Arthur H. Holdsworth for a period of sixteen years, to be auctioned on July 19th 1855.

William Randall was successful in his bid, which was for £775. He was also to pay £50 per annum as long as he employed 6 men (not including rubbish clearers) but if he opened up a fresh part of the quarry and employed 9 men he would pay £75, or for 12 men £100 per annum.

The quarry was well equipped with steam machinery for shafting, pumping and transporting. A tram-way was laid from the quarry across the beach so that barges could be loaded to take away the slate.

William Randall had a cottage at Beesands Cellars and was allowed to build sheds in connection with his business. It is not known how long he worked the quarry, although it yielded good size slates as well as a variety of roofing slates. It closed when it became uneconomical.

DEVONSHIRE.

THE START BAY SLATE QUARRY.

Particulars and Conditions of Sale

OF THE

VALUABLE LEASE,

PLANT AND MACHINERY,

OF THE WIDDICOMB SLATE QUARRY,

KNOWN AS

THE START BAY SLATE QUARRY,

SITUATE WITHIN A QUARTER OF A MILE OF

TORCROSS, in the PARISH of STOKENHAM,

IN THE

COUNTY OF DEVON;

Which will be Sold by Auction, by

Mr. EDWARD LUMLEY,

At the Torcross Hotel, Torcross, near Slapton, Devon,

On THURSDAY, JULY the 19th, 1855, at 11 for 12 o'Clock precisely,

IN ONE LOT,

And if not then Sold, to be divided in Lots, for which see separate Catalogue, which also contains the List of the valuable Stock of Slates and Slabs, and numerous other Effects, which are to be Sold in Lots, at the Quarry, on the 19th of July, at Twelve o'Clock,

By order of the Committee of the above Company.

Particulars of the Lease with Conditions of Sale, and Catalogues of the Property, may be obtained One Week before the Sale at the *Torcross Hotel*, Torcross; of Mr. WM. BUTTERIS, Old Butter Walk, Dartmouth; at the *Seymour Hotel*, Totness; the *Royal Hotel*, Torquay; the *Royal Hotel*, Plymouth; the principal Inns and Hotels in the Neighbourhood of Devon and County of Cornwall; of Mr. LAWE, the Company's Manager, at the Quarry; of Messrs. LUMLEY and LUMLEY, Solicitors to the Company, 41, Ludgate Street, where the Lease may be inspected; and at the Auction Offices, 67, Chancery Lane, London.

THE VALUABLE SLATE QUARRY,

KNOWN AS THE

START BAY SLATE QUARRY,

Is situate on the borders of the Sea, within a quarter of a mile of Torcross, one mile of Slapton, five miles of Dartmouth, fourteen miles of Plymouth, and in the immediate Neighbourhood of other large Towns, and is held under an assignment of a Lease for the unexpired Term of Sixteen Years, from Midsummer last, at the small Royalty of 1-20th, or a Rent Certain of £40 per Annum.

The following is the Inventory of the Plant and Machinery, which will be Sold with the Lease:—

The Twenty-horse-power High Pressure Horizontal Steam Engine, with large Fly Wheel and other Fittings, by Messrs. DAVISON and OUGHTERSON, of Greenock.

The nearly new Twenty-horse-power Wrought-iron Waggon Boiler, with Supply, Waste and Steam Pipes, and the whole of the Brick and Iron Work to same, with Furnace, &c.

The valuable Slate Planing Machine, Jones' Patent, with Driving Wheels, Gear and Apparatus, complete.

The capital Iron Shafting, with Drum to drive same.

The 23-feet Iron Winding Gear, with the whole of the Apparatus, on a Stout Timber Frame.

The very powerful Double Winding Tackle, with Spur Gear, Friction Rollers, Three 203-feet lengths of 2-inch Wrought-iron Chain, &c., with the whole of the stout Deal Framing and Supports.

The Deal Traversing Platform.

The Deal Windlass to work same.

The capital 30-feet Iron Pump, with 6-inch Bore, fitted with Quadrant Motion, Deal Connecting Shafts and Rods, and the stout Deal Framework to support same.

The Wrought-iron Tramway as laid throughout the Quarry to the Sea Shore, on stout Sleepers, about 2350 feet run.

The Five Quarry Waggons and a four-wheel Truck.

The quite new Slate Rubbing Machine, fitted with a 9-feet-6 Iron Bed Plate, &c.

The above Machinery and Plant, which is all nearly new, is of the best Construction, and in every way adapted for Working the Quarry on the most Expeditious and Economical Principles.

The Quarry possesses advantages as regards its Productions, Position, and General Efficiency, not usually to be met with.

It has been established and worked for many Years, much to the advantage of the fortunate holders, and at present possesses every facility for the profitable production of Slate and Slabs.

Two Pits have been recently sunk, and up to the present time have been very productive.

The Slate has obtained a high celebrity, both for its good quality and the large size of the Slabs, and is in great demand in the neighbourhood; and, from the close proximity of the Quarry to the Sea Shore, where Water Transport can be obtained, a large and thriving Trade and ready Market may be made by the Exportation of Slates to London and other large Towns.

The Quarry, being situate on the Sea Shore, forms a ready means of disposing of all the loose Rubble.

To a Public Company, a Capitalist, or any enterprising man, seeking a Property of this description, an opportunity like the present rarely presents itself for the Investment of Capital, with the prospect of large and very satisfactory returns.

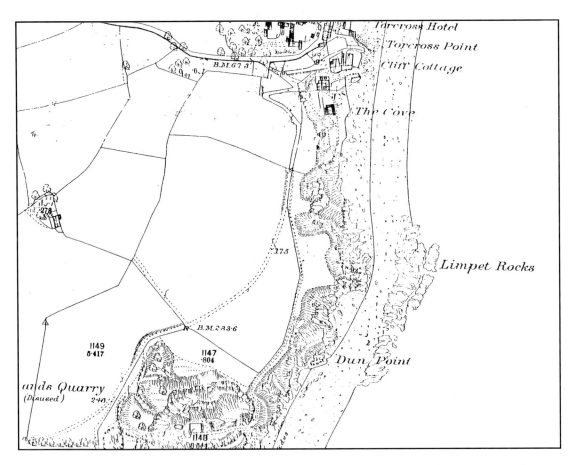

Map of 1886 showing the original coast path at the bottom of Thornhills Field leading down Jacob's Ladder.

Gabriel Putt, head quarryman circa 1881

Start Bay Quarry is now a peaceful bird sanctuary owned by the National Trust.

The narrow entrance from the beach.

All that remains of Jacob's Ladder.

Village For Sale

Torcross was divided between two estates.

The Stokeley Estate owned all the houses at beach level on the sea front excluding the Torcross Hotel. It also owned the Ley and foreshore including the Royal Sands Hotel and many of the farms around Slapton.
In 1898 it all had to be sold to pay off death duties.

The Widdicombe Estate owned the rest of Torcross including Cove House, Cliff House, The White House and most of the houses and land from the hotel to Ley Cliff Cottages along the road towards Kingsbridge. In addition it owned the houses at Widewell, which were all sold out of the Estate in 1921 and 1923.

AN EXCEPTIONALLY CHARMING

FREEHOLD

Residential and Sporting Estate,

KNOWN AS

"STOKELEY,"

A GENTLEMAN'S RESIDENCE

Of moderate size, occupying a charming situation about 50 feet above sea level, and commanding the most beautiful views of the well-known

SLAPTON LEY

IS A LARGE FRESH WATER LAKE.

IT AFFORDS THE BEST OF SHOOTING AND FISHING.

SHOOTING. The Shooting is both varied and good. The natural contour of the land, the nature of the soil, and the undulating and secluded Plantations, intersected as they are by small streams of water, favour, in a remarkable degree, the successful Breeding and Rearing of all kinds of Winged and Ground Game; while the Ley, being the resort of an enormous number of Wild Fowl, including Wild Duck, Tufted Duck, Teal, Widgeon, Mallard, Coot, Moor Hen, Water Rail and Snipe, the sport in this direction is practically unlimited. As an instance of this, it may be pointed out that the bag in Coots alone for one day has numbered some 1,500. The Ley is also the favourite resort of the Bittern and other rare species of Wild Fowl.

FISHING. The Ley affords probably the best Pike Fishing that can be obtained. Baskets of 40 lbs. and upwards have frequently been recorded, one catch in 4 hours reaching 92½ lbs., and consisting of 18 Fish, or an average of 5 lbs. each. Some of the largest Pike caught within the last few years have scaled 29½ lbs., 24 lbs., 20½ lbs., and hundreds approaching that weight. The Perch and Rudd Fishing is equally good, many baskets reaching 400 and upwards. In addition to the above, the Ley also abounds with Eels.

BOATING. First-class Boating may be had, either in the Private Waters of the Ley, which extends over some 180 Acres, or in the open Sea.

YACHTING. The Estate offers great facilities for Yachting, there being good anchorage in Start Bay in fair weather, with Dartmouth Harbour within easy reach.

HUNTING. The Tremlett and South Devon Foxhounds, as also a Pack of Harriers, meet within easy distance of the Estate.

•••

1800s. This etching of the Boxing Day shoot on Slapton Ley shows the Landlord's party in the boats whilst his tenants were allowed around the shores of the Ley. Note that the guns being used are muzzle loading, requiring a rod to push home the powder and shot.

Tenant.	No. on Map.	Description.	Acreage.	Rent.
		PARISH OF STOKENHAM.	A. R. P.	£ s. d.
The Lords Commissioners of the Admiralty		Coastguard Station . . .		10 0 0
The Board of Trade .		Rocket House		2 0 0
Mr. Wm. Perrott .		Fisherman's Arms Inn, and Buildings, stone and cob built and thatched. A fully licensed Public House		15 0 0
Mr. John Pepperell .		No. 1, Lily Terrace, used as a Postal and Telegraph Office . . .		15 0 0
Mr. W. T. Poynter .		No. 2, Lily Terrace . . .		15 0 0
Miss E. Hannaford .		No. 3 ,, ,, . . .		15 0 0
Miss Elizabeth Aitkins .		No. 4 ,, ,, . . .		15 0 0
Mrs. C. Tough .		No. 5 ,, ,, . . .		15 0 0
Mr. Robert March .		No. 6 ,, ,, . . .		15 0 0
		All the Houses in Lily Terrace are of modern construction, built of stone and slated, and are in a good state of repair.		
Mr. J. J. Harwood .		Cottage (stone, cob and thatch) .		9 0 0
,, .		,, ,, ,, ,, .		
Mr. Dawe .		,, ,, ,, ,, .		2 10 0
Mrs. M. A. Gillard .		,, ,, ,, ,, .		2 12 0
Mrs. Ann Chadder .		,, ,, ,, ,, .		2 5 0
Mrs. Blank .	1256	,, ,, ,, ,, .	1 2 9	3 5 0
Mr. Chas. Chadder .		,, ,, ,, ,, .		2 12 0
Mr. J. Clements .		,, ,, ,, ,, .		3 3 0
Mrs. M. G. Patey .		,, ,, ,, ,, .		2 0 0
Mr. W. Harwood .		,, (stone and cob built, and part thatched and part slated) . . .		5 0 0
Miss Elizabeth Beel .		Commodious Dwelling House (stone and cob built and slated) . . .		35 0 0
Mr. J. R. Gill .		Cottage (stone, cob and thatch) .		11 0 0
Mr. James Kelland .		,, (stone, cob and slated) .		2 12 6
Mrs. Sarah Rogers .		,, ,, ,, ,, .		2 12 0
Mr. P. Hutchings .		Site of Cottage (ruins) . .		0 2 6
Mr. Wm. Vickery .		Cottage (stone, cob and slated) .		2 12 0
Mr. George Kelland .		,, (stone, cob and thatched) .		3 10 0
Mr. George Pepperell .		,, ,, ,, ,, .		3 5 0
		The Reversion in Fee of Leases of the undermentioned Dwelling Houses, held by the Tenants for terms certain of 63 years from Lady-day, 1848.		Conventionary Rent.
Mrs. Elizabeth Pepperell .		Dwelling House (stone, cob and slated)		1 0 0
Mr. Henry Worth .		,, ,, ,, ,, ,,		1 0 0
		The annual letting value of these houses is estimated at £40 each		
Mr. Isaac Dare .	Pt. 1282	Frontage alongside Road and Ley .	0 2 1	1 5 0
		Total . .	A. 2 0 10	£213 6 0

A Singularly Productive Agricultural Holding,

SUITABLE IN EVERY RESPECT FOR A HOME FARM,

And situate immediately to the east of the Mansion and Grounds, about 1 mile from Torcross, and half-a-mile from Stokenham. The property is known as

STOKELEY FARM,

AND COMPRISES

A STONE AND SLATED FARM HOUSE,

Containing 2 Sitting Rooms, Kitchen, Back Kitchen, Dairy, Pantry and about 7 Bed Rooms.

THE FARM BUILDINGS

Are chiefly constructed of stone with slated roofs, and are arranged round a Fold Yard. They include 4 Cow Sheds, 3 Cattle Pens, Pound House, with Apple Chamber over and Cider Cellar underneath, open Cattle Shed, Stabling for 7 Horses, Nag's Stable for 2, Corn and Straw Barn, with a Root House at each end. There are also a Cart Shed and double Trap House adjoining, 6 Cow Houses with Root House at end, timber and slated Granary and a row of 8 lean-to Piggeries. In Enclosure numbered 1361 on Sale Plan is a stone and thatched Store Shed, with Cattle Shed underneath.

In Enclosure numbered 1429 on Sale Plan is

A PAIR OF STONE AND THATCHED COTTAGES,

Each containing 4 Rooms, together with Garden and double Piggery. There is also a Set of Buildings, comprising a stone and thatched Range, including Cattle Shed with Barn over, Root House and another stone and thatched open Cattle Shed. In No. 1338 is

A STONE AND SLATED COTTAGE,

Containing 4 Rooms and Basement.

The above, together with the productive Pasture and Arable Land,

extends over an area of about

253a. 2r. 24p.

THE HIGHLY VALUABLE PROPERTY,

KNOWN AS

THE "ROYAL SANDS" HOTEL,

Situate adjacent to the main road leading from Torcross to Dartmouth, about 1½ miles from Torcross, 8 miles from Kingsbridge, and 7 miles from Dartmouth. It includes

A FULLY-LICENSED HOTEL,

Built of stone, and containing full-sized Billiard Room, with Lavatory and Water Closet adjoining; Coffee Room, Sitting Room, Smoking Room, Bar, 13 Bed and Sitting Rooms, 2 Water Closets; together with Kitchen, Beer Cellar, Wash House, Scullery, Larder and 2 Store Rooms.

THE OUTBUILDINGS

Are conveniently situated near the House, and comprise 4-stalled Stable, Harness Room with Loft over, Loose Box and Store Room.

Around a second Yard is a stone and thatched Range of 4 Piggeries, 5-stalled Stable, Coach House, 3 Poultry Sheds and lean-to Coal Shed.

The above, together with the Arable and Pasture Land, extends over an area of about

21a. 0r. 16p.,

3 w

SOUTH DEVON.

PARTICULARS, MAP AND CONDITIONS OF SALE

OF

AN ATTRACTIVE

Residential and Unique Sporting Property

KNOWN AS

THE STOKELEY ESTATE,

Situate about 7 miles from Dartmouth, 6 miles from Kingsbridge and 20 miles from Torquay. The Great Western Railway service is available either at Kingswear or Kingsbridge, and hence London may be reached in about 6 hours. The Property, which extends over an area of about

1,257 ACRES,

COMPRISES

A GENTLEMAN'S RESIDENCE

Of moderate size, occupying a charming situation, commanding the most delightful views of the proverbially interesting Slapton Ley, with Start Bay and the English Channel beyond.

THE PLEASURE GROUNDS

Abound with choice Shrubs and Ornamental Trees in a high state of maturity, and include

A TENNIS LAWN and excellent FRUIT and VEGETABLE GARDENS, with ORANGE HOUSE;

Good Stabling Accommodation for Eight Horses,

With Coach House and Groom's Rooms. The Estate includes

FIVE FARMS, each having a suitable Homestead.

THE "ROYAL SANDS" HOTEL,

With STABLINGS and OUTBUILDINGS, also ENCLOSURES OF ACCOMMODATION LAND,

The LARGER PORTION of the HOUSES and COTTAGES forming the VILLAGE of TORCROSS,

A number of judiciously placed GAME COVERTS, WOODS and PLANTATIONS, and the renowned

SLAPTON LEY.

The Estate comprises the Lordship of the Manor or reputed Manor of Stokenham, with its Rights, Privileges, and Chief Rents,

The whole (including a fair estimate for the Lands in hand) produces a Rental value of about

£2,226 PER ANNUM:

MESSRS.

WALTON & LEE

Have received instructions to offer the above for Sale by Auction,

AT THE MART, TOKENHOUSE YARD, LONDON, E.C.,

On TUESDAY, the 7th day of JUNE, 1898,

AT TWO O'CLOCK PRECISELY

(Unless previously disposed of by Private Treaty).

Copies of these Particulars may be had of Messrs. EARDLEY HOLT, HULBERT & HUBBARD, Solicitors, 28, Charles Street, St. James' Square, London, S.W.; Mr. H. J. D. PARSONS, Estate Agent, Bampfylde House, Exeter; or of the AUCTIONEERS, at their Offices,

10, Mount Street, London, W.

VACHER & SONS, PRINTERS, WESTMINSTER.

3 K

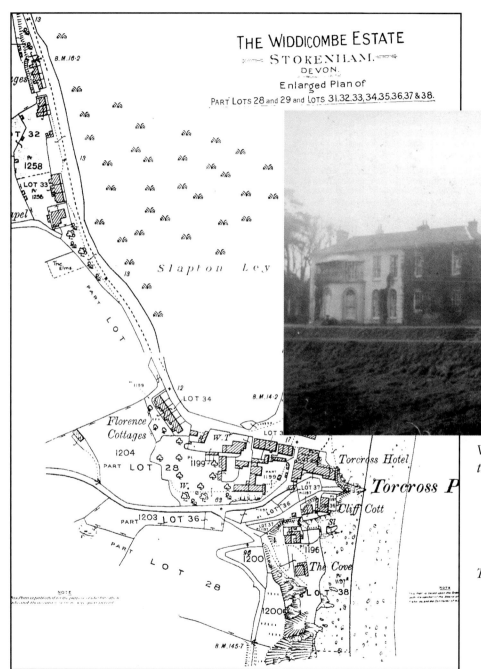

THE WIDDICOMBE ESTATE

STOKENHAM.
DEVON.

Enlarged Plan of

PART LOTS 28 and 29 and LOTS 31,32,33,34,35,36,37 & 38.

1921
Start Bay
on the South Devon Coast
— The —
Wiiddicombe Estate
Stokenham

Widdicombe House did not form part of the sale.

The parts of Torcross included in the sale.

35

SALE OF PROPERTY.

WIDDICOMBE ESTATE, STOKENHAM.

"It is with great regret we see resident landlords of large estates selling them," said Mr. Rendell, of the firm of Rendell and Snwdye, Newton Abbot, at the sale of Widdicombe Estate, Stokenham, at the Town Hall, Kingsbridge, on Monday afternoon. "Unfortunately," added Mr. Rendell, "the majority of them are good landlords whose loss from the district they should feel very much. They were only sorry they felt compelled to sell their property. He felt convinced that they could ill afford to lose Capt. Holdsworth from their district. (Applause.) If England only consisted of such good landlords as Captain Holdsworth, very little fault would be found with them, and he knew he had shown himself to be a good sportsman." (Applause.)

The property offered comprised the freehold agricultural and sporting property known as the Widdicombe Estate, covering about 925 acres. Lot one included the fine Queen Ann residence, "Widdicombe House," the residence that has been the family seat of the Holdsworth family for a long number of years. The woods, plantations and covers, offers exceptional sporting facilities, and Widdicombe Ley, noted for its coarse fishing and wild fowl shooting. Also Lower Widdicombe Farm, over 230 acres, in the occupation of Mr. A. Ellis; "Sunnydale," a pleasantly situated dwelling house at Beesands Cellars, and eight cottages. The whole is about 370 acres. This was put up in one lot, but not a single offer was received and was withdrawn.

Lot 2 was Mattiscombe Farm 48 acres, about 24 acres, chiefly arable, having been taken off and put in the first lot. It included three cottages, and the whole let at £105 a year. Mr. F. Rowe is the tenant of the farm. Bidding was started at £1,600, and Mr. W. Beer became the purchaser for a client at £2,700.

Stokenham Barton, 186 acres, in the occupation of Mr. W. H. Pearse, with farmhouse, buildings, and four cottages, commanded fair competition. The bidding was started at £4,000 and steadily rose to £6,600, Mr. Groom, of Torcross, being the purchaser.

The highest offer received for a stone-built cottage at Widewell was £240, and the property was not sold.

There was very keen competition for another modern cottage at Widewell, in the occupation of Mr. F. W. Spencer, and let at £16 13s. The opening offer was £250 and quickly advanced to £515, Mr. Wells, a visitor, being the purchaser. A small cottage at Widewell was purchased by the tenant, Mr. Perrin, for £250.

£370 was the highest offer received for the wheelwright's and blacksmith's shops with two dwelling-houses with gardens at Carehouse-cross, which was not accepted, the property being withdrawn.

Island Farm, 51 acres, with house and buildings, was purchased by Mr. J. H. Brooking, Kellaton, for £2,450.

Lot 16 was a stone and thatched cottage in the village of Stokenham. The highest offer was £75, which was not accepted. A stone and slated cottage, in the occupation of Mr. E. Crimp, was bought by Mr. Patey, Torcross, for £250. Three stone and thatched cottages in the village, were sold to Mr. W. H. Wakeham for £130.

"The Tradesmen's Arms," with 2 cottages and garden, the whole rented at £22 15s., was started at £300, and at £500 Mr. Veale, of Dartmouth, became the purchaser.

Mr. Groom purchased a cottage for £100 and 2 cottages with gardens for £150. A block of 4 cottages with shoemaker's shop and gardens was sold to Mr. F. A. Brooking, Kingsbridge, for £185.

Lower Beeson Farm, 60 acres, with house and buildings, was sold to the tenant, Mr. H. Foale, for £2,250. The tenant, Mr. R. Rogers, of Higher Beeson, 45 acres, also purchased his farm at £1,500.

Seventeen acres of arable land at Beeson was sold to Mr. Hill for £300. Mr. T. Honeywill purchased the next two lots, 8 and 15 acres of arable land, for £200 and £300.

Mr. J. Hannaford, Torcross, gave £1,750 for the butcher's shop, dwelling-house, buildings, and 19 acres of land, that he occupies.

The highest offer received for the Torcross Hotel, a fully licensed house, with two cottages and stables, was £3,000, and the lot was not sold.

Eleven acres of accommodation land at Torcross, was purchased by Mr. Groom for £600.

There was keen competition for cottage property at Torcross. "Lea Cliff," four excellent stone cottages, let at £22 15s. a year, was started at £400 and was sold to Mr. Pillar for £630.

The next lot, two cottages and gardens adjoining, was sold to one of the tenants, Mr. E. Mabin, for £300.

"Ley View," three stone cottages, received an opening bid of £600 and went up to £900, when Mr. Hutchings, a tenant, was declared to be the purchaser. A row of six well-built cottages, known as "Florence Cottages," let at £30 10s. a year, was started at £500 and at £10 bids went up to £910, when Mr. Hurrell, of Dartmouth, became the purchaser.

Five cottages, with shop and bakehouse, near the hotel, was sold for £1,000 to Mr. Johnson, Torcross. The highest offer received for "Cliff Cott," a pleasant seaside residence, was £880, and it was withdrawn.

"Start View," a small marine residence was purchased by the tenant, Miss St. Aubyn, for £730.

"The Cove," a small marine residence at Torcross Point, with cottage and gardens adjoining was started at £800. It was sold to Mr. Tucker for £1,060. £1 5s. ground rent on "The Elms" was purchased by Mr. E. Sanders for £40. The trustees of the Congregational Church, Torcross, purchased the ground rent of three guineas on their property for £62 10s. The total result of the sale was £28,907.

Messrs. Masterman and Everington, of London, and Mr. A. M. Davson were the solicitors, and Messrs. Hingston and Son, Totnes, the land agents.

LOT 38.

(Coloured Dark Blue on Plan No. 1 and also on Enlarged Plan No. 8).

THE BEAUTIFULLY SITUATED

SMALL MARINE RESIDENCE

AT TORCROSS POINT.

known as

"THE COVE"

with Cottage adjoining known as "Cove Cottage,"

together with **Gardens, Cliff** and **Foreshore,** the whole extending to

2 Acres 2 Roods 10 Poles,

with uninterrupted Views of Start Bay.

'THE COVE' is in the occupation of M. St. Aubyn, Esq., on a quarterly tenancy at the annual Rental of £80 (Tenant paying Outgoings). The Residence is Stone built and Slated, with the top part of the walls Slate hung, is approached by a Drive Entrance, and is protected by a Verandah in the front and on the North End, and comprises : Entrance Hall, Front Sitting Room with Tiled Grate and Marble Mantel, another Front Sitting Room with Grate and Marble Mantel, Kitchen with Range, Scullery with Furnace, and Larder. On the First Floor are 4 Bedrooms, Box Room, Bath Room with Bath (H. and C.) and W.C. There are Pretty Gardens with Paths to Summer House on Cliff and to the Beach.

There is Small Yard, Stone and Slated Trap House with Loft over, 2-Stall Stable and Harness Room, and Slated E.C. Water is laid on from the Village supply, and there are Two Gardens on the West at the top of the Cliff.

COVE COTTAGE is Stone and Slated and contains 3 Rooms downstairs and 3 upstairs, and E.C. with Garden in front. Water is laid on from the Village supply. This Cottage is in the tenancy of H. M. Marriott, Esq. for a term of 5 years expiring at Michaelmas, 1921, at the annual Rental of £8 0s. 0d.

The Public have a right to approach the Beach by the stone steps in this lot.

SCHEDULE.

No. on Ord. Map.	DESCRIPTION.				A.	R.	P.
Pt. 1196	**In occupation of M. St. Aubyn, Esq.** The Cove, Gardens, Cliffs, &c. ..		..	..	} 0	3	16
Pt. 1196	**In occupation of H. M. Marriott, Esq.** Cove Cottage and Garden ..		..	..			
	In Hand.						
1200a	Garden ..	..	..	..	0	1	18
1200	Do. ..	..	..	..	0	0	31
Pt. 1197a	Foreshore ..	..	..	..	1	0	25
					A 2	2	10

LOT 36.

(Coloured Dark Green on Plan and also on Enlarged Plan No. 8).

THE PRETTY

SEASIDE RESIDENCE

known as

"CLIFF COTT"

Situate at the summit of Torcross Point and commanding uninterrupted Views of the wide expanse of Start Bay and the English Channel.

The Residence is Stucco and Slated and of pleasing elevation, and contains : 3 Reception Rooms, Kitchen, Scullery, Small Room, 4 Bedrooms, Bath Room with Bath (H. and C.), and W.C., and is fitted with Double Windows on the Sea side. At the Rear is Small Yard with Outhouses. There is a nice Front Garden with Soft Water Tank and Summer House thatched with Ley Reeds, together with **Gardens** across Road and a prettily laid-out

Garden with Tennis Lawn of 0a. 2r. 20p.

close by, the whole extending to

0a. - 3r. - 28p.

and in the occupation of Dr. Todd for 3 years from September 29th, 1919, with option to continue by giving 3 months' notice previous to the end of the third year, at the annual Rental of £50 (Tenant paying Rates).

SCHEDULE.

No. on Ord. Map.	DESCRIPTION.			A.	R.	P.
Pt. 1197	**In occupation of Dr. Todd.** Cliff Cott and Gardens ..	..	..	0	1	2
1203	Gardens and Tennis Lawn ..	..	..	0	2	20
				0	3	22
Pt. 1197	**In occupation of W. Blank, rent free for cleaning up.** Garden on East of Cliff Cott Garden ..		..	0	0	6
				0	3	28

LOT 29.

(Coloured Yellow on Plan No. 1 and also on Enlarged Plan No. 3.)

The Fully Licensed Residential Hotel

known as the

"TORCROSS HOTEL"

Together with Commodious Stabling, Gardens and Pasture Field

the whole extending to an area of

7a. - 0r. - 24p.

situate at Torcross and occupying an unrivalled position in the centre of Start Bay, with the far-famed Slapton Sands and Slapton Ley adjoining, 8 miles from Dartmouth and 7 from Kingsbridge, with a frequent Motor Omnibus Service between these Towns.

THE HOTEL

is substantially built of Stone, Stucco and Slated. There is a Paved Court Yard facing the Sea and a Verandah. The accommodation is as follows :—Large Glazed Lounge Entrance, Entrance Hall, Private Bar and Office, Large Side Bar with Serving Hatch from Private Bar and Cellar beneath ; Sitting Room, 23ft. 9in. x 19ft. x 9ft. 6in., with Tiled Grate and French Windows to Verandah ; Coffee or Dining Room, 37ft. 6in. x 17ft. 4in. x 9ft. 6in., with Fireplace and Serving Hatch to Kitchen ; Sitting Room, 15ft. x 15ft. 9in. x 9ft. 6in., with Bay Window and Tiled Grate ; Billiard Room, 15ft. 7in. x 24ft. 8in. x 9ft. 6in., with one Bay and one other Window ; Kitchen with large Range ; Scullery with Furnace and Washup ; Coal House with Store Room over ; Larder and Store Room ; Lumber Room over Kitchen ; W.C. and 2 Servants' Bedrooms, W.C. and 2 Lavatory Basins.

The First Floor comprises : Sitting Room with Bay Window and Balcony ; Sitting Room, also with Bay Window and Balcony, and **Twelve Bedrooms,** 2 W.C.'s, and Bath Room with Bath (H. and C.), and Lavatory Basin (H. and C.), Mangle Room with large Linen Cupboards.

On the Second Floor are **Fifteen Bedrooms,** 2 W.C.'s, and Bath Room with Bath (H. and C.)

LOT 35.

(Coloured Red on Plan No. 1 and also on Enlarged Plan No. 3).

A BLOCK OF

5 Well-built Stucco and Slated Cottages

together with

DWELLING HOUSE, SHOP & BAKEHOUSE,

situate at Torcross, close to the Torcross Hotel.

No. 1 Cottage is rented by Mr. H. B. Bartlett on a monthly tenancy at the annual Rental of £6 0s. 0d. (Landlord paying Rates), and contains 2 Downstair and 4 Upstair Rooms, Outhouse, and hand-flushed Closet at back.

Nos. 2, 3, 4 and 5 Cottages are rented by the Lord Commissioners of the Admiralty on a quarterly tenancy at the apportioned Rent of £47 per annum (Tenants paying Rates), the Gardens being Part of Lot 31.

Nos. 2 and 3 contain 2 Downstair and 2 Upstair Rooms, with Outhouses and hand-flushed Closets at the back.

Nos. 4 and 5 contain 2 Downstair Rooms, 3 Upstair Rooms, with Washhouses and W.C.'s at the back.

THE DWELLING HOUSE AND SHOP

is in the occupation of Mrs. E. Carter on a half-yearly tenancy at the annual apportioned Rental of £26 15s. 0d. (Landlord paying Rates), and comprises : Front Shop, Back Sitting Room with Grate, Entrance Passage, Front Sitting Room, Kitchen with Range. On the First Floor are 5 Bedrooms and W.C., and above are 2 Attics. At the Rear is Bakehouse with Loft over, Outhouse and hand-flushed W.C., Washhouse and Furnace, and a Side Entrance.

This Lot will be sold with the right to drain into the cesspit in the Hotel Stable Yard (Lot 29), as at present enjoyed.

LOT 28.

(Coloured Brown on Plan No. 1 and also partly shewn on Enlarged Plan No. 8).

The Butcher's Shop, Dwelling House,

BUILDINGS, SLAUGHTER HOUSE

AND

LAND

Situate at TORCROSS

and occupied by Mr. Hannaford at the apportioned annual Rent of £84, on a half-yearly tenancy, the whole extending to

29a. 0r. 8p.

The Dwelling House and Shop is Stone, Stucco and Slated, and is approached through a large Front Garden and has a Vegetable Garden at the side, and comprises Butcher's Shop (the Fittings are the property of the Tenant), Sitting Room, Kitchen, Dairy, Coal House, 7 Bedrooms, and W.C., Coal House, Cake House over Dairy, and Lean-to Store Room.

Adjoining the Road is Galvanized Iron Piggery and Yard, and Stone and Slated 2-Stall Stable (let to Mr. L. Guest at £2 12s. per annum), and Trap House with Loft over this and Stable.

At the Rear in the Orchard is Thatched Waggon House, Slated Root House, Thatched 4-Stall Cow Shed and Loft over, Large Yard, Slated Cellar and Trap House, 8-Stall Stable, and Engine Shed with Loft over, and Galvanized Cart Shed, Slated 5-Stall Cow Shed and Loose Box with Loft over, Galvanized Iron Root House, Galvanized Wood Shed, and Galvanized Washhouse with Furnace, and 4 Piggeries and E.C. In the Orchard is Well supplying water to this Lot and also to Florence Cottages (Lot 84), and this Lot is sold subject to such supply as now enjoyed, and to the general supply of water to other Lots at Torcross.

In No. 1204a is Stone and Slated Slaughter House with Paved Floor and Water laid on, and 2 Fasting Houses with Loft over.

(**Note.**—The Fittings in the Slaughter House are the property of the Tenant).

SCHEDULE.

No. on Ord. Map.		DESCRIPTION.				CULTIVATION.		A.	R.	P.
	1188	Higher Long Field	..	..	..	Arable	..	2	3	31
	1189	Lower Do.	..	..	..	Do.	..	2	3	26
	1191	Higher Three Corners	..	..	..	Pasture and Water	..	2	3	2
	1192	Higher Putcombe	..	..	..	Arable	..	2	3	32
	1207	First Field	..	..	..	Pasture and Water	..	2	2	36
	1206	Lower Putcombe	..	..	..	Arable	..	1	3	7
	1205	Grove	..	..	..	Pasture and Water	..		2	20
	1202	Pope's Hill	..	..	..	Arable	..	2	3	1
	1204	Lower Three Corners	..	..	..	Pasture	..	1	1	21
	1204a	Do. and Slaughter House	..	..	..	Do.	..		2	6
Pt.	1199	House, Shop, Buildings and Orchard, &c.			..	Orchard. &c.	..	1	2	2
	1208	Knowle	..	..	..	Arable	..	6	0	24
								A 29	0	8

LOT 33.

(Coloured Dark Blue on Plan No. 1 and also on Enlarged Plan No. 8).

3 EXCELLENT, STONE, STUCCO & SLATED COTTAGES

known as

"LEY VIEW."

situate at Torcross, adjoining the Congregational Chapel and facing Slapton Ley and the Sea, and occupied as follows :—

The South Cottage let to Mrs. Pepperell on a half-yearly tenancy at the annual Rental of £16 0s. 0d. (Landlord paying Rates), and containing 4 Downstair Rooms, Back Kitchen, 4 Bedrooms, Outhouses, W.C. and Garden.

The Middle Cottage in the occupation of Mrs. Hutchings on a half-yearly tenancy at £14 0s. 0d. per annum (Landlord paying Rates), and having similar accommodation, with Tailor's Workshop at rear, W.C. and Garden. (*Note.*—The Greenhouse is the property of the Tenant).

The North Cottage is let to Miss Brooking on a half-yearly tenancy at £18 7s. 0d. per annum (Landlord paying Rates), and contains 4 Downstair Rooms, Back Kitchen, 4 Bedrooms, Garden and W.C.

The whole being Part Ordnance No. 1258, and estimated to contain **0a. 1r. 18p.**

LOT 34.

(Coloured Dark Blue on Plan No. 1 and also on Enlarged Plan No. 8).

A ROW OF SIX WELL-BUILT STONE & SLATED COTTAGES

known as

"FLORENCE COTTAGES."

situate at Torcross, facing Slapton Ley and the Sea, with Gardens in front, each containing 2 Downstair Rooms and 3 Bedrooms, Washhouse and E.C., with Yard at rear.

No.						£ s. d.			
1	is occupied by	Mr. W. Diamond	on a monthly tenancy	apportioned at		4 15 0	p.a. Landlord paying rates.		
2	,,	Mrs. Tomlinson	,, ,,	,,	,,	5 15 0	,, Tenant	,,	,,
3	,,	Mr. Wm. Stone	Half-yearly	,,	,,	4 15 0	,, Landlord	,,	,,
4	,,	Mr. G. Stone	,, ,,	,,	,,	5 15 0	,,	,,	,,
5	,,	Mrs. Rogerman	monthly	,,	,,	4 15 0	,,	,,	,,
6	,,	Mr. Lewis Guest	half-yearly	,,	,,	4 15 0	,,	,,	,,
						30 10 0			

This Lot is Part Ordnance No. 1199, and is estimated to contain **0a. 1r. 18p.**

This Lot is sold with the benefit of the Right of Water Supply from a well on Lot 28, as now enjoyed.

The Gardens to these Cottages form part of Lot 31, and the Rent has been apportioned in respect thereof.

This Lot is sold with the benefit of the Water Supply from a spring on Lot 1, as now enjoyed and with the benefit of the right to enter on Lots 1, 8 and 29, to cleanse, repair, renew or relay the line of Pipes.

Torcross, watercolour by Rev. John Swete, 1793.
Houses from left to right – The Old Chapel – Sea Breeze – Start Lea – Port Cottage – Thrift Cottage and Prideaux Farm.

The Rocket House was the most northerly building in the village, it was used to store the breeches-buoy rocket and lines and other equipment for the coastguards.

The post on the right of the photo was one of two on the shingle ridge set one nautical mile apart, the second one being positioned near the Royal Sands Hotel. There were two more posts on high ground on the inland side of the Ley in line with, and the same distance apart, as those on the foreshore. Boats were able to test their logs by lining up each pair and measuring the distance between the pairs. (See page 134).

1890. The Coast Guard House (now part of the Sea Shanty Restaurant and flats), was the dwelling of the head coastguard. Each morning and evening the duty coastguards would parade to raise or lower the flag.

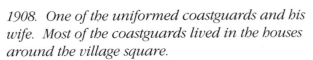

1908. One of the uniformed coastguards and his wife. Most of the coastguards lived in the houses around the village square.

1925. The large wooden structure of the Crowing Cock tea room and restaurant now dominates the approach to Torcross from Slapton Line.

The bungalows on the hill above the village were built by Mr Robert Garner before he built the Greyhomes Hotel.

1930. The interior of the Crowing Cock. The tables are laid with fresh flowers, ready for the arrival of the coach trade. The proprietor would sit behind the wood and glass screen at the cash desk. From this vantage point he or she could supervise the service and collect the money from the waiting staff.

Crowing Cock Café, 1929. On hot summer days cream teas were served outside. Perhaps fresh eggs were also available from the cafes own hens.

Two well-to-do ladies are being escorted to the seats by their chauffeur in full uniform.

1932. Business for the Crowing Cock was so good that more space was needed. A wooden hut was purchased from the First World War air field at Prawle and rebuilt to the south of the coastguard house.

1932. The Crowing Cock owned two wooden structures, the Rocket House and the Coastguard House. The Greyhomes Hotel was completed in 1930 and can be seen on the hill above the inn.

1890. The Fisherman's Arms (now the Start Bay Inn) would have been a simple hostelry for the local fishermen, probably serving the locally brewed 'White Ale' or strong cider produced from the many local apple orchards.

1950s. Now the Start Bay Inn, but the present car parking area still owned by Mrs Gyllenship. A small walled beer garden was provided for the changing expectations of the clientele.

1960s. Pubs were by now beginning to serve a greater variety of food.. The owners of the Start Bay Inn built a café in the beer garden area. This was destroyed in the storm of 1980.

1892. Lily Terrace from the beach. Note the enclosed stern of the fishing boat. This prevented the boat being swamped when the fishermen returned to the beach with their catch and gave some shelter whilst fishing in bad weather.

1930s. Back view of the beach houses from Lily Terrace to Startlea House. The reeds around the Ley were cut and used as thatch.

1869. View taken from near the Fisherman's Arms before Lily Terrace was built. The first house on the right of the picture is Sea Cottage.

1892. Sea Cottage with the post office (now Bay House) as part of Lily Terrace.

Harwoods Shop (on the site now occupied by Waterside House).

One of the cottages belonged to an old retired sailor, Bill Patey, and his even-older invalid cousin Emma Skinner. The cottage in the picture was the home of widow-lady Alice Harwood and her teenage son Ken. Alice's late husband William had been a cobbler by trade, repairing shoes in his shop beside the cottage and supplementing his income by fishing in the bay. His boat, a large clinker-built seiner, worked straight off the beach, and during the winter he would pull it off the shingle and keep it between the buildings. After William died Alice turned the shop into a general store where, besides a huge selection of essentials, she sold delicious ice-cream which she made from rich, yellow, Devon milk.

1948. Port Cottage was one of the first fishermen's cottages in the village and has survived attempts to destroy it. First in 1940 it narrowly escaped the German bomb which destroyed Harwoods shop next door, then in 1978 nature had a go and nearly succeeded when the sea undermined its foundation (see page 96).

1896. Harwoods shop and the front entrance to Startlea House, which at the time was a second home for the Chrisford family who took their annual holidays in the village.

1920s. Bay View and Startlea House.
On the early maps Startlea House is referred to as Parade House. It can be clearly distinguished on the front cover of this book, and has had a variety of uses over the years.

Possibly it was built as a Dower house for one of the local manors. It was later owned by a series of wealthy second home owners until in the 1930s it became the home of the local doctor who converted the fisherman's store shed behind it into a surgery for his patients. Then in 1954 it was purchased by the owners of the Torcross Hotel and was used for many years as an annex to accommodate the guests of the hotel.

Startlea House (to the right)
In 1973 Denis and Mary Rogers (owners of the Torcross Hotel) closed it as an annex and converted it into a private House.

In 1988 Mary sold it to her daughter and son in law, who now once more welcome visitors for bed and breakfast.

1929. Looking over Torcross from the view point up Widewell Lane. The houses in the foreground have just been completed by local builder Harry Sanders, who built most of the houses in Homeleigh Road.

1932. View of the doctor's surgery behind Startlea House.
Swans Nest, as it is now known, is at present used for self catering holiday accommodation.

1892. Two fishermen's cottages stood on the plot of land now occupied by Venture House. Holding Ground and Sea Breeze look the same as they do today.

One of the cottages has fallen into disrepair and has been pulled down, and the old two-man winch for the boats has gone.

1920s. Both fishermen's cottages have been replaced with the Venture House.

The Torcross fishing fleet has been reduced in numbers, but you can still see the nets being dried on the beach.

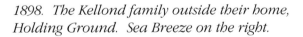

1898. The Kellond family outside their home, Holding Ground. Sea Breeze on the right.

1865. Painting by William Collingwood-Smith (RWS). Showing the original chapel with Cliff House above it.

1875. The chapel has been enlarged to accommodate the school room for the village children.

1835 drawing by W .H. Way (Royal Academy artist) who used to stay in the village. The three little girls in the picture are Mary, Susan and Kezia Pike.

1890. The hotel was owned by Mr W. Vickery who started the Dartmouth Coaching Company when he owned the Royal Sands Hotel. This picture shows the central block of the hotel, which was built first, attached to one of the original fishermen's cottages. This cottage was demolished in 1894 to make way for the wing which now incorporates the hotel bar.

1920s. Photo of the hotel fully built and as you would recognise it today. One of the bathing machines advertised on the building in the photo above can be seen on the beach. It must have been very difficult to push up and down the beach on those wheels.

1894. The hotel has become more popular and has increased in size and a new wing has been added, incorporating the old school room and chapel.

The cliff path did not go up the steps beside the chapel, but went around the cliff, below the coastguard lookout.

1900. The original cliff path around the cliff to Cove House. It fell into disrepair and in 1939 a gun emplacement was built over it.

1918. Torcross Hotel dining room using oil lamps before electricity was supplied to the village in 1935. The residents lounge was through the door behind the head waiter.

1950s. The hotel was owned by Denis and Mary Rogers at this time.

This early aerial photo (probably taken from a biplane) shows the southern end of the cliff path by Cove House. The middle section on the point has already collapsed.

1950s. A World War Two gun emplacement has been built at the end of the old path, above the tunnel outlet that drains Slapton Ley.

1820 print by T. H. Williams of Cliff House, at which time it was probably still in the possession of the 'Home Missionary Society'.

Cove House was formally the 'Dower House' for Widdicombe House, and was sold off in 1921 to pay death duties.

1918. The White House before the annex was built. The owners of Cove House built a thatched summer house on the cliffs in their garden.

The White House with annex which was completed in 1938.

The Centre of the Village

1899. Changing the horses outside the hotel ready for the trip into Kingsbridge.

The three cottages between the hotel and the shop were occupied by the coastguards and their families.

Dare's shop sold everything from china to groceries. Parking in the square does not seem to be a problem!

1901. View across the Ley showing one of the fisherman's cottages where Venture House now stands. Nothing has yet been built on the site of the present Fuchsia Pottery.

1908. The stone posts that still stand on the verge of the bend by Florence Cottages were linked by chain. This was removed during the Second World War to help the war effort and has never been replaced.

In 1854 Welsh miners were brought in to dig the tunnel, through the cliffs to the other side of the headland, to control the water level of the Ley, which would flood the village, making the road impassable during the winter months. At the same time a weir was built across the tunnel entrance, to increase the overall depth of the Ley, and to prevent the water level dropping in the long dry spells.

1918. View from the Square towards Florence Cottages. Note that no houses have yet been built in the field behind the cottages.

1922. Domestic geese were allowed to graze the banks of the Ley but needed to be attended. One of these young 'goose-girls' was Doris Hibbs who in later life ran the bar in the Torcross Hotel.

In 1919 Robert Garner, the grandfather of the present owner of Greyhomes Hotel, was travelling from Dartmouth to Salcombe to purchase property there. He had to change buses at Torcross and wait for a connection to East Portlemouth. While he was waiting he walked up the hill and came across Pope's field belonging to Edward Hannaford. A shaking of hands sealed the deal and Robert never completed his journey to Salcombe. The name 'Greyhomes' was taken from the 1912 Irish ballad – 'My little Greyhomes in the west'. The bungalows were started in 1920 and the hotel was completed in 1929.

Greyhomes Hotel nearing completion.

1936. View of the backs of the houses and Hannaford's yard. The small barn to the right of their yard was the original slaughter house.

The barn on the road next to Florence Cottages is where Lewis Guest used to stable his horse for his carrier business.

1938. People are still taking holidays believing that war was not possible.

1929. The Post Office had moved from Lily Terrace by the beach, and now had a prominent position in the centre of the village.

The Venture House has also been built on the site of the older fishermen's cottages.

1932. New glazed porches for both the house and the Post Office, with its lovely thatched roof.

1936. *The top floor of the Post Office caught fire, destroying the thatched roof and most of the interior. The roof was replaced with modern materials, and the shop was revamped and enlarged with a new extension and shop window.*

1950s. *The tourist trade once again begins to flourish with the ending of petrol rationing after the war. Property is being renovated and a mood of optimism grows after the hardships of the last decade.*

1899. View of Torcross taken from a position near to the boat house which was situated close to where the 'Pick-your-own' farm shop is situated at the present time.

The thatched boat house offered winter shelter for some of the rowing boats used to fish the Ley.

Perch, rudd and pike were plentiful and large. Specimens of pike over 35lb were not uncommon, and the popularity of the Ley as a fishing lake lasted until the Ley and its surroundings were purchased by Herbert Whitley and became the property of Whitley Trust, who later leased it off to the Field Centre.

1889. Cliff House, the White House, Torcross Hotel, the cottages and shop in the square, Prideaux Farm, the small stable and barn and Florence Cottages were all part of the Widdicombe estate at this time and belonged to the Holdsworth family. Mr Holdsworth built Florence Cottages and Lea Cliff Cottages in 1880 and Lea View Cottages in 1894.

1894. Lea View Cottages, next to the chapel, Little Aish, Myrtle Cottage and Lea Cliff Cottages at the end of the village also formed part of the Widdicombe estate.

The hard packed, unsealed road surface must have been very dusty in dry weather for those houses alongside.

1902. Bicycles have become more popular as a leisure pursuit although the uneven road surface must have made the ride a little uncomfortable.

1918. The Elms was built close to the chapel near the boundary of the Torcross Field, which contained several majestic trees after which the house was named. It was built in 1913 by Edward Sanders and his son Harry, the site having been purchased some years previously from F. J. Holdsworth Esq.

Torcross

1921. The whole of Torcross Field in the foreground. The woods on the hill behind it were bought at the sale of the Widdicombe Estate by Edward Sanders' son Wilfred for £550 while he was still in the Royal Air Force and based in Egypt.

The small barn behind the hedge on the right of the picture was used as a slaughter house for Hannaford's butchers from the 1950s to the 1980s.

1929. Harry Sanders developed the field and built the houses along Homeleigh Road.

Horse and cart are still being used to transport materials as a cheaper alternative to motorised transport.

In 1883 the site of the Congregational Chapel was leased from the Widdicombe Estate by the trustees of the chapel for 99 years at an annual rent of three guineas.

The commemorative stone on the east wall of the building was laid by Martin Sparkes Esq. On 18th October 1883. When completed, the total cost of building was £500.

The trustees were able to buy the freehold of the land on 4th April 1922.

1924. Edward Sanders bought a piece of land next to the Elms from his son Wilfred for the sum of £40. He then built the garage workshop and petrol station that can be seen to the left of the picture.

1907. Back of Chapel and thhe allotments and gardens behind Lea View Cottage.

1925. The tennis court and small pavilion on the flat area behind the chapel. This was owned by the Chrisford family who also owned Startlea House around that time.

1897. Lea Cliff Cottages were the last houses of the village on the road to Kingsbridge. They were built in 1880 by Frederick John Holdsworth of Widdicombe House. Mrs Chadder, seen here with her family, used to keep domestic geese on the banks of the Ley.

The Inland Dwellings

View over the top of Prideaux Farm (now Hannaford's butchers) showing corn stooks in the field behind Florence Cottages, and allotments in the field behind Lea Cliff terrace.

The newly built chapel is behind the trees in the foreground. The large amount of reed in the Ley was removed in the 1920s by positioning two traction engines, one on either side of the Ley, and dragging a large scoop between the two. If this had not been done the Torcross end of the Ley would look like the reed beds of the Gara Valley at Strete Gate.

1935. The Silver Jubilee of King George V was enthusiastically celebrated by the residents of Torcross. In the photo Florence Cottages indicates how the rest of the village would have looked.

1935. Lewis Guest, Taffy Sutton and George Dure put the finishing touches to a celebration arch they erected across the road by Florence Cottages.

1963. View over the area behind the chapel. The tennis court has gone and one or two houses have been built in its place.

1972. After Chris Venmore took over the garage from Mr Garrett, he developed the forecourt of Torcross garage to incorporate the show room in the photo, from where Chris had a very successful car sales agency.

The Changing Uses of the Beach

1897. The Torcross fishing fleet was as numerous as the present day's leisure craft. It was hard work for both the men and for their wives.

The heavy wooden boats would be pushed down the beach on wooden blocks called 'ways' and put in the water before anybody boarded. In the days before rubberised boots, it was essential for the men to start the day with dry clothing, so their wives would literally pick the men up and carry them into the water alongside the boat and then lift them over the gunnels into the craft.

Helping to haul up the boat at the end of the day was also part of the day's work for the hard working wives of the fishermen. This picture was taken at Hallsands, but it illustrates the point.

1895. There were large numbers of fish to be caught in Start Bay at the turn of the century. One of the fishermen would stand on the top of the cliff to spot the shoals. He would then signal the waiting fishing boat and direct it where to lay its net. One end of the net would be left on shore and then the boat would circle the shoal of fish, playing out the net as it went. The boat would then be rowed back to the beach and all hands, including the wives, would haul the net onto the beach and then the catch would be divided between all those who had helped.

1898. Modesty was all important, so the bathing machine on wheels would be pushed down the beach to the water's edge so any ladies wishing to go for a swim could step straight into the water and they would not be seen in their bathing costume.

Even those sitting on the beach did not expose much skin.

1920. Swimwear was not very practical and certainly did not help the wearer to swim through the water smoothly. Many of the costumes were made of wool and when wet they would become heavy and sag in all the wrong places.

1920. The wooden boarding on large wheels was a moveable jetty that could be manouvered into the water at any stage of the tide so that guests of the hotel could be taken for boat trips without getting wet. It was still fashionable to keep well covered up when reclining on the beach.

Torcross Regatta may have had its origins in rivalry between the various fishing communities of Start Bay and nearby coastal settlements over particular areas of the sea shared for their livelihoods. Co-operation was necessary in making up crews of gigs and other boats, therefore any bad feeling by the fisherman could be overcome by friendly competition as they raced each other at the regatta (Harold Fox's *Evolution of Fishing Villages*).

1939 was the last time Torcross Regatta was held. The photo shows what a good turn out there was for the event. The paddle steamer The Duchess of Devonshire had made a trip from Dartmouth to join in the day's fun. The official starter for the races was Edward Hannaford, the local butcher, who you can see in the bottom left hand corner of the photo with a shot gun under his arm to use as the starting gun.

1902. Whenever the weather permitted, The Duke of Devonshire paddle steamer or the Duchess of Devonshire would bring visitors to Torcross from Dartmouth across Start Bay.

1904. Passengers disembarking from the Duchess of Devonshire to have afternoon tea at the Torcross Hotel.

1970s. Sun worshippers crowd the beach with their wind breaks. A good sun tan is essential to prove you had a good holiday!

Glass fibre boats have taken over from the traditional wooden, clinker built boats and powerful outboard motors have taken the place of oars and sails.

Robin Rose-Price was one of the first to have a ski boat off the beach. Apart from mono skiing most afternoons when he was not on duty at the Torcross Hotel, he would often be seen performing this trick on a round disk, which was towed by the boat. Ken Small is the driver in this instance.

June 1st 2002. The Queen's Golden Jubilee weekend, the residents of Torcross enjoyed the first Regatta since 1939.

The first shore-based race of the afternoon was the obstacle race.

Photo shows Benny and Matty Vowles racing to the finishing line. A gold medal was given to every child in the village just for taking part.

2002 Regatta.
The boats were all lined up for the water activities. The swimming races were completed, but unfortunately only two boat races were staged. The sea became too rough, much to the disappointment of everyone taking part.

Water filled balloons were given to the children to throw at the participants of the adult obstacle race.

The men's sack race saw one disqualification. One competitor had misunderstood the rules and used two sacks, (one on each leg).

The volleyball competition.

The day ended with everyone bringing their own food to cook on the barbecues, supplied by the regatta committee.

Extreme Weather Conditions

1911. The coach road between the houses and the beach was built on a bed of beach slates with a sloping seaward face. This had proved more than adequate until the government of the day gave permission for Sir John Jackson, contractor of Devonport Docks in Plymouth, to remove 395,000 cubic metres of shingle from the beach at Hallsands.

Dredging began in April 1897 and continued until the winter of 1902. On average 1,600 tonnes of shingle were removed every day during this period.

1917. The same storm that destroyed twenty four houses at Hallsands also raged against Torcross. The reduced level of the beach allowed the waves to break closer to the houses and to the beach road. The road was washed away in several places, exposing its base of beach slate which had been placed there so many years previously.

1917. The houses avoided serious damage on this occasion but from then on the inhabitants needed to barricade their windows whenever there was an easterly gale, as shown in this photo of the old Post Office in Lily Terrace.

1929. The 1917 storm also undermined the main road just north of the Rocket House, between what is now the 'Tank car park' and the beach. This was very effectively repaired using interlocking sheet metal piles then capping them with a bevelled low profile concrete top, to allow the waves to pass harmlessly over it. It is still doing its job after 85 years!

1951. The worst damage to that date was inflicted on Torcross.

Several days of strong south-easterly winds had removed the beach in front of the houses and deposited it on the shore at Strete Gate. The sea wall and road were completely undermined, causing the road to collapse.

1951. The most severe damage to the road was between the hotel and Startlea House where the beach was at a lower level.

1952. The decision was made to use a similar designed defence as used for the 1918 wall. Sheet piling was driven into the beach to prevent further undermining of the houses.

1952. This repair work held firm and protected the houses behind it, even in the storm of 1979 which so badly damaged the other houses outside its protection.

1963 saw the worst winter for snow since the blizzards of 1947. The narrow lanes around Torcross were blocked and the Ley froze over. The village square became a playground for building snowmen as there were no cars moving around.

1976. The glorious long hot summer was not without its problems. The streams feeding the Ley dried up and the water evaporated completely from the fresh water lake. It was possible to walk across the Ley on the hard baked mud, although there were still a few soft spots in the middle!

1978–1979 storm. This photo was taken by Peter Jones at the height of the storm on the morning of 31st December 1978. The severe gale force easterly winds had coincided with the highest spring tides of the year, causing the mountainous waves to pound the houses and to wash shingle and boulders across the A379 main road.

1978. It was impossible to approach the seafront by using the alleyways. The waves rushed down them at waist height and with such force that people risked being washed off their feet.

1978. At low tide the next day it was possible to inspect the damage. Those houses that were not protected by the 1952 wall had been undermined by the drop in the beach level.

Waterside House shown here was lucky to escape collapse.

Port Cottage, belonging to Bill Marsh the coast guard, was not so lucky. It lost three of its outside walls during the first night, shown here, and suffered further collapse at the next high tide, leaving the roof suspended, and twisting and buckling in the gale force winds.

1978. The cedar wood structure of the Start Bay Café was pounded by the waves and flattened, leaving the roof in the middle of the pub's car park and the pool table nearly washed into the road.

1978. This enormous hole appeared in the promenade in front of the hotel. The earth and debris filling, which supported the surface, had been sucked out of the cave at the bottom of the hole and then the pressure of the water had smashed the concrete on the surface. Luckily no-one was there when it happened!

Men and equipment were slow to arrive in Torcross because the heavy snow fall had blocked all the roads.

The first bulldozer to arrive was driven by Lewis Elliot. He had battled his way on foot along the cliff path through deep snowdrifts to get a bulldozer from Beasands. The lanes were impassable, even for a tracked vehicle, so Lewis undertook the extremely hazardous journey across the open fields and over the headland to bring his bulldozer to the rescue of Torcross.

The emergency repair work is clearly visible from the end of the 1952 wall to the Rocket House, the northern most building on the seafront. The diggers could only work when the tide went out so progress was slow.

1978. Rocks and debris were hastily pushed in front of the threatened houses to prevent further undermining.

The forces of nature gave a four day break for these temporary repairs before unleashing another storm to batter Torcross.

This photo was taken in December 1979. The boulders used for the emergency repairs were dug out from in front of the houses and piled half way down the beach to form a barricade so that work could continue at all tides. A vast trench was then dug to get down to the working level before the steel piles were driven into the shingle.

1980 February. The tops of the steel piles were capped and reinforced beams were laid to the footings of the wave return wall which now separates the promenade from the beach.

2nd April 1980. The Queen and the Duke of Edinburgh visited Torcross to see how the work was progressing.

1980. The concrete was poured into the shuttering to form the reinforced bracing and to create the wave return wall. The gap between the beams was then filled with protruding boulders which were concreted in place. These boulders break up the power of the waves if the beach level is low at any time.

Laurie Emberson was presented to the Queen. The village of Torcross owe a huge vote of thanks to Laurie and to the other members of the Sea Defence Committee, Dennis Rogers, Paddy Tye, Roger Jefferis and Paul Lansdale. Without Laurie's diplomacy and untiring efforts, Torcross would still have a boulder defence and not a permanent sea wall as can be seen at the present time.

Sarah Rose-Price and Clare Stubbs presented bouquets to the Queen outside the Torcross Hotel.

Brownies, Guides, Cubs and Scouts formed a guard of honour for the Queen's visit.

The War Years in and around Torcross, 1939–1945

On the 27th November 1940, at 9.45pm, a German bomb dropped in the yard behind Harwood's shop. The explosion flattened the buildings around it. The Harwood family escaped without serious injury. It is said that the thatched roofs remained intact when the walls collapsed and fell like a huge tea-cosy over the people below, showering them with dust and spiders, but saving their lives.

This pile of rubble is all that remained of Harwood's shop after the blast. A replacement was not built until 1951. This is where Waterside House now stands.

Another view of the bombed site on the right of the photo, after it had been cleared away. For several years there was just an open space between Port Cottage and Startlea House.

1942. Two other bombs were dropped on Torcross before it was taken over by the Americans in 1943. The first one landed harmlessly in the Ley close to the reeds opposite the end of Homeleigh Road.

The second bomb was dropped from low level in the dark and landed on the hillside below Cove Ark. The back-blast of this explosion lifted all the slates off the roofs from Handicraft Cottage to the barns in Hannaford's yard. Margaret Hannaford is checking to see if her car has been damaged.

IMPORTANT MEETINGS

The area described below is to be REQUISITIONED urgently for military purposes, and must be cleared of its inhabitants by DECEMBER 20th, 1943.

Arrangements have been made to help the people in their moves, to settle them elsewhere, and to advise and assist them in the many problems with which they will be faced. To explain these arrangements

PUBLIC MEETINGS

will be held as follows:

FRIDAY Nov. 12th
11 a.m.
EAST ALLINGTON CHURCH
2-30 p.m.
STOKENHAM CHURCH

Earl Fortescue, M.C., The Lord Lieutenant
in the Chair.

SATURDAY Nov. 13th
11 a.m.
BLACKAWTON CHURCH
2-30 p.m.
SLAPTON VILLAGE HALL

Sir John Daw, J.P., Chairman Devon County Council
in the Chair.

These general meetings will be immediately followed by special meetings to discuss the problems of farmers, who are requested to remain behind for them.

IT IS VITALLY IMPORTANT to every householder that he should arrange to attend whichever of these meetings is nearest to his home, and where necessary employers of labour are requested to give their work-people time off for this purpose.

THE AREA AFFECTED

ALL LAND AND BUILDINGS lying within the line from the sea at the east end of Blackpool Bay in Stoke Fleming parish to Bowden; thence northward along the road to the Sportsman's Arms; thence west along the Dittisham-Halwell road to the cross-roads ¼-mile east of Halwell village; from this cross-road along the Kingsbridge road to the Woodleigh-Buckland cross-roads; thence along the road Buckland, Frogmore, Chillington, Beeson and Beesands to the sea, but excluding the villages of Frogmore, Beeson and Beesands. The roads forming the boundary are outside the area.

The parishes involved are the whole, or almost the whole, of Blackawton, East Allington, Sherford, Slapton and Strete, most of Stokenham, and parts of Stoke Fleming, Buckland-tout-Saints and Halwell.

MORTIMER BROS. PRINTERS AND PUBLISHERS, TOTNES

4th November 1943
The chairman of Devon County Council, Sir John Daw, was ordered to requisition an area of 30,000 acres as shown on the map opposite. This included the villages of Torcross, Stokenham, Chillington, Frogmore, Sherford, East Allington, Blackawton, Slapton and Strete. It also included 180 farms and many small hamlets. It effected 750 families and totalled 3000 men, women and children.

12th November 1943
Notices having been posted, the first public meeting was held at East Allington. The following day further meetings were held at Blackawton and Slapton. People were ordered to leave their houses and farms which in some cases families had occupied for generations, taking with them all their possessions including their farm animals and pets.

There was very little protest as this was war time, but it was difficult for some to understand especially the elderly and the farmers who had to leave crops in the ground knowing that there was a desperate shortage of food in Britain.

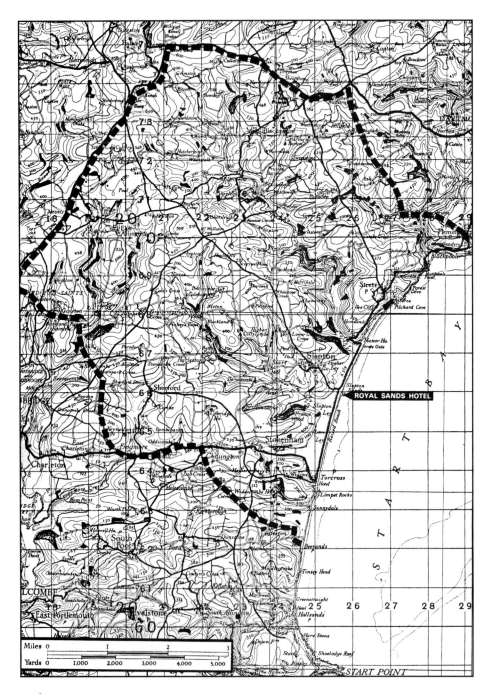

Early December
The evacuation was well under way. Packing cases and boxes had been provided and extra manpower where needed.

The Admiralty informed the church commissioners that the safety of the church valuables could not be guaranteed. So all the carved screens and pulpits were taken down and carefully packed away, along with any other artifacts
.

The first of the American soldiers started to arrive and out of kindness handed out sweets to the local children who had not seen such treats for several years because of food rationing. Also it was the first time many of the locals had seen a coloured person.

20th December 1943
The area had been evacuated of its civilian population, and the American troops moved into their homes. One American veteran, on a recent visit to Torcross, said "We were not told that the houses were to be returned to their owners, we thought that they were to remain in the possession of the army. If we had known we would have taken greater care of them".

Torcross was turned into a fortress. A barbed wire fence was erected along the foreshore and back to the Ley. A minefield was laid in the area between the road and the Ley (where the 'Tank' car park is now located). Roadblocks were set up where the road passed through the barbed wire and in front of Hannaford's butcher shop. Anti tank pillars were built in the water of the Ley to stop them going round the roadblocks. Concrete gun emplacements and pillboxes were built and anti-aircraft guns were placed near the Start Bay Inn.

A closer view of the barbed wire defence along the seafront.

One of the concrete bunkers built onto the Crowing Cock Café, facing Start Point, another was built inside the restaurant, facing down Slapton beach. Other gun emplacements are still to be found on either side of the headland by the hotel and there is still one inside the hotel's boat shed.

VIEW OVER TORCROSS.

9606T.J.V.

Hannaford's yard and orchard were used as a tank park. All three of the barns in the foreground were pulled down by the Americans to make enough room for the tanks. You can imagine what the Hannaford family felt when they were finally allowed back into their home!

This letter shows that damage to property in the evacuated area was no accident during 'Excercise Tiger'.

SUPREME HEADQUARTERS
ALLIED EXPEDITIONARY FORCE
G-3 Division

SHAEF/23036/8/Trg   19 April 1944.

Subject: Exercise Tiger.

To:

    1. Exercise TIGER will involve the concentration, marshalling and embarkation of troops in the TOR BAY - PLYMOUTH area, and a short movement by sea under the control of the U.S. Navy, disembarkation with Naval and Air support at SLAPTON SANDS, a beach assault using service ammunition, the securing of a beachhead and a rapid advance inland.

    2. Major troop units are the VII Corps Troops, 4th Infantry Division, the 101st and 82nd Airborne Divisions, 1st Engineer Special Brigade, Force "U" and supporting Air Force units.

    3. During the period H-60 to H-45 minutes, fighter-bombers attack inland targets on call from the 101st AB Div and medium bombers attack three targets along the beach. Additional targets will be bombed by both fighter-bombers and medium bombers on call from ground units. Simulated missions will also be flown with the target areas marked by smoke pots.

    4. Naval vessels fire upon beach obstacles from H-50 to H-hour. Smoke may be used during the latter part of the naval bombardment both from Naval craft by 4.2" chemical mortars and at H-hour by planes, if weather conditions are favourable. Naval fire ceases at H-hour.

    5. The schedule of the exercise is as follows:

      22 April   Move to marshalling area commences.

D-Day 27 April   101st AB Div simulates landing. Preparatory bombardment by air and navy. Assault landing and advance of 4th Div.

      28-29
      April   Advance of 4th Div & 101st AB Div continues. 82nd AB Div simulates landing, secure and holds objective.

      (Exercise terminates on 29 April)

    6. Joining instructions will be issued later.

                  W. R. PIERCE,
                  Colonel, G.S.C.,
      TOP SECRET   Chief, Training, Sub-Section.
This paper must not be taken out of this Headquarters except as laid down in Para. 27, SHAEF Inter-Division Standing Security Regulations dated 9 February 1944.

From a painting by S/M Ted Archer 1995. Photograph by kind permission of Ian Davidson. www.friendsofthelaurel.co.uk

2.00am on 28th April 1944
Seven fast German E-boats came across the convoy and torpedoed LST 507 and LST 531 One other LST received a hit, but was able to make it back to Dartmouth. The rest of the LSTs continued with the planned assault of Slapton Beach. 749 dead is the official figure of men lost in the attack, but this number is believed to be greater.

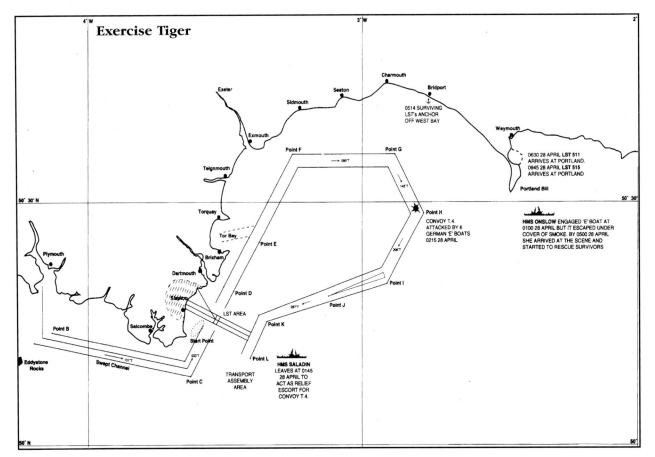

The Convoy left Plymouth escorted by a destroyer HMS Scimitar, and a corvette HMS Azalea. Unfortunately HMS Scimitar was rammed by one of the landing craft and holed, so she had to return to Plymouth. HMS Azalea continued along as the convoy headed into Lyme Bay to give the soldiers the same time at sea as they would have to experience if they crossed the Channel to France. The second problem was that all the convoy had received orders with a typing error, giving the wrong radio frequency. So they were using the wrong frequency to communicate with HMS Azalea or with HQ ashore. When the flotilla of seven German E-boats were spotted on the radar of a destroyer off Portland Bill, there was no way to warn the LSTs in the convoy.

*28th April 1944 Targets on the beach and further
inland were attacked by both fighter bombers
and by medium bombers. At the same time the
Naval vessels open fire at selected targets.
To make it more realistic the defenders were
using live ammunition throughout the assault.
200 more lives were lost to 'friendly fire' during
the practice landings.*

*The infantry were the first to secure the
beachhead.*

Once the beach-head was secured, men and equipment were landed to continue the fighting inland.

More infantry being transported to the beach by Strete Gate.

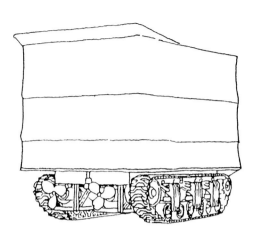

Although some of the tanks were driven off the ramps of the LST directly onto the beach, many were launched well out to sea so as not to endanger the landing craft.

To make the Sherman tank amphibious, a canvas apron was erected on metal supports. Although the tank was below the surface of the water, the tank crew remained dry as long as the waves did not splash over the rim of the apron.

Sketch by kind permission of Ray Freeman 'We Remember D-Day'.

LSTs landing heavy equipment directly onto Slapton beach. As the days practice continued, more men and machinery continued to be brought ashore.

The full scale of Exercise Tiger can be appreciated from the number of vessels within Start Bay, standing off Slapton beach.

When the fighting was over, the men still had to be fed. The army catering corps also needed to practice under battle conditions.

The engineers also needed to refine their skills, so a pontoon bridge was built across the Ley from the site of the bombed Royal Sands Hotel to the shore on South Grounds Farm.

The ruins of the Royal Sands Hotel. The story is that a minefield had been laid around the hotel, when a stray dog walked into the area and set off one of the mines. However the large crater in the picture shows that at least one bomb and probably a great many naval shells landed on or near the hotel.

U.S. troops marching past the ruined Royal Sands Hotel.

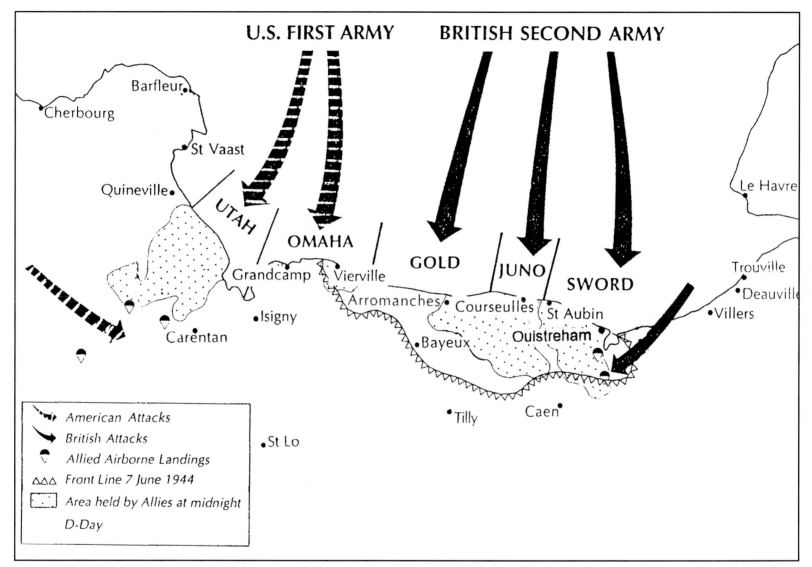

6th June 1944
The men that trained on Slapton Beach and in the evacuated area, were engaged in the attack on Utah and Omaha beaches.
Casualties on Utah beach numbered 200, probably less than a tenth of those who lost their lives in Exercise Tiger.

Map by kind permission of Ray Freeman 'We Remember D-Day'.

Austin C. Chestnut from Ohio was later killed in France, but not before his tank destroyed three enemy tanks. He died 9th July 1944.

This inscription was found on the windowsill of Windfalls house in Torcross. The U.S. tank driver had been billeted in the house during the evacuation of its civilian owners.

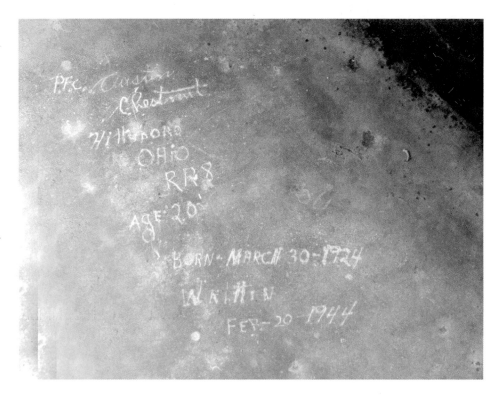

Pocket Book

A SHORT GUIDE TO

GREAT BRITAIN

WAR AND NAVY DEPARTMENTS
Washington, D. C.

INTRODUCTION

YOU are going to Great Britain as part of an Allied offensive—to meet Hitler and beat him on his own ground. For the time being you will be Britain's guest. The purpose of this guide is to start getting you acquainted with the British, their country, and their ways.

America and Britain are allies. Hitler knows that they are both powerful countries, tough and resourceful. He knows that they, with the other United Nations, mean his crushing defeat in the end.

So it is only common sense to understand that the first and major duty Hitler has given his propaganda chiefs is to separate Britain and America and spread distrust between them. If he can do that, his chance of winning *might* return.

No Time To Fight Old Wars. If you come from an Irish-American family, you may think of the English as persecutors of the Irish, or you may think of them as enemy Redcoats who fought against us in the American Revolu-

1

A pocket book was issued to every American soldier once his ship had left port to cross the Atlantic.

Some of the other headings on the following few pages

Age instead of size
'You will come across the British pride in age and tradition'.
Remember there's a War on
'British trains are cold because power is needed for industry'.
The British like sports
'Cricket will strike you as slow in comparison to American football'.
Indoor Amusements
'A great place for recreation is the "pub". The beer is now below peacetime strength, but can still make your tongue way at both ends'.
Keep out of Arguments
'You can rub a Britisher up the wrong way by telling him "We came over and won the last one for you"'.

tion and the War of 1812. But there is no time today to fight old wars over again or bring up old grievances. We don't worry about which side our grandfathers fought on in the Civil War, because it doesn't mean anything now.

We can defeat Hitler's propaganda with a weapon of our own. Plain, common horse sense; understanding of evident truths.

The most evident truth of all is that in their major ways of life the British and American people are much alike. They speak the same language. They both believe in representative government, in freedom of worship, in freedom of speech. But each country has minor national characteristics which differ. It is by causing misunderstanding over these minor differences that Hitler hopes to make his propaganda effective.

British Reserved, Not Unfriendly. You defeat enemy propaganda not by denying that these differences exist, but by admitting them openly and then trying to understand them. For instance: The British are often more reserved in conduct than we. On a small crowded island where forty-five million people live, each man learns to guard his privacy carefully—and is equally careful not to invade another man's privacy.

So if Britons sit in trains or busses without striking up conversation with you, it doesn't mean they are being

2

haughty and unfriendly. Probably they are paying more attention to you than you think. But they don't speak to you because they don't want to appear intrusive or rude.

Another difference. The British have phrases and colloquialisms of their own that may sound funny to you. You can make just as many boners in their eyes. It isn't a good idea, for instance, to say "bloody" in mixed company in Britain—it is one of their worst swear words. To say: "I look like a bum" is offensive to their ears, for to the British this means that you look like your own backside. It isn't important—just a tip if you are trying to shine in polite society. Near the end of this guide you will find more of these differences of speech.

British money is in pounds, shillings, and pence. (This also is explained more fully later on.) The British are used to this system and they like it, and all your arguments that the American decimal system is better won't convince them. They won't be pleased to hear you call it "funny money," either. They sweat hard to get it (wages are much lower in Britain than America) and they won't think you smart or funny for mocking at it.

Don't Be a Show Off. The British dislike bragging and showing off. American wages and American soldier's pay are the highest in the world. When pay day comes, it would be sound practice to learn to spend your money according to British standards. They consider

3

AT HOME in America you were in a country at war. Since your ship left port, however, you have been in a *war zone*. You will find that all Britain is a war zone and has been since September 1939. All this has meant great changes in the British way of life.

Every light in England is blacked out every night and all night. Every highway signpost has come down and barrage balloons have gone up. Grazing land is now ploughed for wheat and flower beds turned into vegetable gardens. Britain's peacetime army of a couple of hundred thousand has been expanded to over two million men. Everything from the biggest factory to the smallest village workshop is turning out something for the war, so that Britain can supply arms for herself, for Libya, India, Russia, and every front. Hundreds of thousands of women have gone to work in factories or joined the many military auxiliary forces. Old-time social distinctions are being forgotten as the sons of factory workers rise to be officers in the forces and the daughters of noblemen get jobs in munitions factories.

But more important than this is the effect of the war itself. The British have been bombed, night after night and month after month. Thousands of them have lost their houses, their possessions, their families. Gasoline, clothes, and railroad travel are hard to come by and incomes are cut by taxes to an extent we Americans have not even approached. One of the things the English always had enough of in the past was soap. Now it is so scarce that girls working in the factories often cannot

get the grease off their hands or out of their hair. And food is more strictly rationed than anything else.

The British Came Through. For many months the people of Britain have been doing without things which Americans take for granted. But you will find that shortages, discomforts, blackouts, and bombings have not made the British depressed. They have a new cheerfulness and a new determination born out of hard times and tough luck. After going through what they have been through it's only human nature that they should be more than ever determined to win.

You are coming to Britain from a country where your home is still safe, food is still plentiful, and lights are still burning. So it is doubly important for you to remember that the British soldiers and civilians have been living under a tremendous strain. It is always impolite to criticize your hosts. It is militarily stupid to insult your allies. So stop and think before you sound off about lukewarm beer, or cold boiled potatoes, or the way English cigarettes taste.

If British civilians look dowdy and badly dressed, it is not because they do not like good clothes or know how to wear them. All clothing is rationed and the British know that they help war production by wearing an old suit or dress until it cannot be patched any longer. Old clothes are "good form."

One thing to be careful about—if you are invited into a British home and the host exhorts you to "eat up—there's plenty on the table," go easy. It may be the family's rations for a whole week spread out to show their hospitality.

Waste Means Lives. It is always said that Americans throw more food into their garbage cans than any other country eats. It is true. We have always been a "producer" nation. Most British food is imported even in peacetimes, and for the last two years the British have been taught not to waste the things that their ships bring in from abroad. British seamen die getting those convoys through. The British have been taught this so thoroughly that they now know that gasoline and food represent the lives of merchant sailors. And when you burn gasoline needlessly, it will seem to them as if you are wasting the blood of those seamen—when you destroy or waste food you have wasted the life of another sailor.

British Women At War. A British woman officer or noncommissioned officer can—and often does—give orders to a man private. The men obey smartly and know it is no shame. For British women have proven themselves in this war. They have stuck to their posts near burning ammunition dumps, delivered messages afoot after their motorcycles have been blasted from under them. They have pulled aviators from burning planes. They have died at

the gun posts and as they fell another girl has stepped directly into the position and "carried on." There is not a *single record* in this war of any British woman in uniformed service quitting her post or failing in her duty under fire.

Now you understand why British soldiers respect the women in uniform. They have won the right to the utmost respect. When you see a girl in khaki or air-force blue with a bit of ribbon on her tunic—remember she didn't get it for knitting more socks than anyone else in Ipswich.

23

124

Autumn 1944. Work started to clean up the area ready for the civilian population to return. Buildings had to be made safe and any unexploded ordnance disposed of. The workforce comprised the Militia.

In this photo, the army camp beds have been removed from the hotel and stacked in the courtyard. Many of the doors inside the hotel had been removed and burnt for firewood to keep the troops warm over the winter months.

The thatched roofs of The Venture House and The Haven have been destroyed by fire.

The Manor House Hotel at Strete Gate was also used as target practice. The damage was so severe that it was never rebuilt and is now the picnic area on the corner where the A379 leaves the beach to start its ascent to Strete, by the car park.

These buildings also belonged to the Manor House Hotel, but were situated on the other side of the road beside the Ley. They were repaired and now form part of the lovely house that can be seen at Strete Gate.

24th July 1954
The dedication of the Monument presented by
the United States Army in gratitude to the people
of the South Hams.

Present at the dedication of the Monument were Lieutenant General
John Lee, Commanding General of the Communications Zone,
European Theatre of Operations and Sir John Daw, chairman of Devon
County Council, who had the job of explaining to the local population
why they had to leave their homes in 1943.

Fifty years on a Royal Marine Sounds the 'Last Post' at the commemoration service held by the Sherman tank in the Torcross car park.

The Sherman tank that lay on the seabed for forty years

Divers from the British Diver's boat 'Zodiac' attached two 10 tonne lifting bags to the tank while it was on the seabed.

Ken and Anne Small accompany the tank in an inflatable boat as it is dragged through the shallow water by a one inch thick cable attached to a 100-tonne pull Leyland truck up on the road, with a 27-tonne Caterpillar bulldozer part way down the beach with a heavy duty pulley block to increase the efficiency of the pull.

The tank is finally out of the water, and the drag up the beach commences with the tank's tracks apparently locked solid after forty years of salt-water corrosion.

However, as the tank touches the concrete slipway at the end of the promenade the tracks began to turn as if they had only just been serviced.

Slapton Cellars

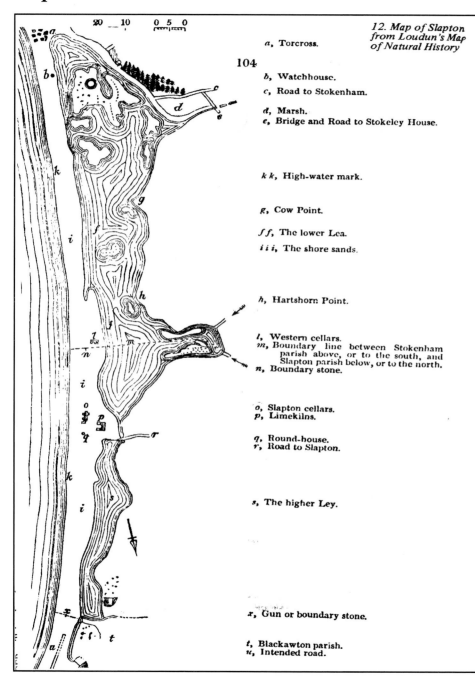

20 __ 10   0 5 0

104

12. Map of Slapton from Loudun's Map of Natural History

a, Torcross.
b, Watchhouse.
c, Road to Stokenham.
d, Marsh.
e, Bridge and Road to Stokeley House.

k k, High-water mark.

g, Cow Point.
f f, The lower Lea.
i i i, The shore sands.

h, Hartshorn Point.

l, Western cellars.
m, Boundary line between Stokenham parish above, or to the south, and Slapton parish below, or to the north.
n, Boundary stone.

o, Slapton cellars.
p, Limekilns.

q, Round-house.
r, Road to Slapton.

s, The higher Ley.

x, Gun or boundary stone.

t, Blackawton parish.
u, Intended road.

Around 1602 Slapton was protected by a drawbridge across the Ley on the site of the present road bridge.

Fish was an important part of the villager's diet and by 1737 fishermen's store huts were built at The Cellars on the foreshore.

Once the coast line was made safe from plundering, these huts would have been made more permanent and become dwelling houses. By 1800 records show that there were three cottages, and a causeway down the beach for landing coal and limestone for the three lime kilns.

In 1831 an inn was built alongside the cottages, the inn-keeper being one John Stabb. This inn later became known as the Sands Hotel. In 1855 King Edward V11 stayed at the inn and granted it permission to be called the Royal Sands Hotel.

1854. A decision was made to build a coast road between Dartmouth and Kingsbridge. The only route before this was via Coles Cross and Bowcombe Bridge. To achieve this it was necessary to control the flood waters which regularly opened gaps in the shingle ridge. A tunnel was built by Welsh miners through the cliff at Torcross to take away the excess water

In 1856 the new road was opened by Governor Holdsworth of Dartmouth and Widdicombe House above Torcross.

The Royal Sands Hotel

1854. The Sands Hotel with the new coast road on its way to Torcross in the distance.

Mid nineteenth century artist's impression of the Royal Sands Hotel with formal gardens.

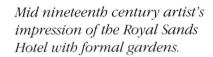

The Slapton Ley & Sands Hotel near Dartmouth

View of the hotel with fishermen's store huts on the beach. The causeway across the Ley that would at one time have lead to the drawbridge.

ROYAL SANDS HOTEL

Path from the hotel to the boats on the shore of the Ley passes the ruins of the old lime kilns.

ROYAL SANDS HOTEL SLAPTON

1900s. The hotel had become renowned for the fresh water sports of fishing and shooting. As it prospered, a large glass roofed extension was built onto the Torcross end of the original inn.

The small post with the triangle on the top on the right of the photo is one of the pair that mark the end of the measured nautical mile. The other pair being at Torcross.

View of the hotel and the new extension from across the Ley.

Slapton. Royal Sands Hotel.

HAVING fished the waters of Slapton Ley on many occasions it is indeed a pleasant task to write these few lines for the benefit of any Angler who may contemplate an attack on the inhabitants of that wonderful water—of Rudd and Perch there must be literally millions in the Ley—these supply ample bait for the Pike fisher and not a few goodly specimens will come to the net of any Angler who fishes for them specially.

It is the Pike, however, which claim the special attention of most Slapton Anglers—Slapton Ley may justly be called a Pike Anglers' Paradise and has yielded many a twenty pounder. It is well nigh impossible to draw a blank at Slapton and it is not uncommon for an Angler to run a score of fish before lunch. The boatmen are good fellows who know their business and the best of Pike Anglers in Great Britain fish this water.

In the most beautiful surroundings, hard by the sea and at the foot of the hills, you could take no more peaceful yet exhilarating holiday than with a rod and line at Slapton.

These waters are preserved and controlled by the Proprietress of The Royal Sands Hotel, where every convenience and comfort is offered to Anglers and their families. Year by year veterans of the rod return to this haven of sure sport.

E. MARSHALL HARDY.

The Hotel Brochure

THE HOTEL FROM THE BEACH (1)

ONE OF THE BEDROOMS (3)

SLAPTON LEY FROM THE HOTEL (2)

A CORNER OF THE DINING ROOM (4)

Engraving by G.C. Leighton Brothers
1868. It is possible that the house on the shore is part of Strete Undercliff, but there is no reference on
the picture as to its location. Local people know that there was a village on the beach in the vicinity
of Strete Gate but as there are no signs today of any ruins or foundations nobody know exactly
where it was located.

The ruins behind the boat and below the cliffs at Strete Gate could be the lost village of 'Strete Undercliff'.

Original watercolour by Payne

The Manor House Hotel

1928. *The Manor House Hotel at Strete Gate was situated at the northern end of Slapton Sands with magnificent views across Start Bay. It has now been pulled down and is the picnic site next to the car park.*

1937. *The hotel was so successful that a new wing was added to nearly double the number of bedrooms.*

1932. South elevation of the hotel with the glass conservatory for use when it was too cold to take afternoon tea on the veranda.

1932. Looking up the drive to the main gates. This entrance is still visible as you drive up the hill, just past the walled vegetable garden, now a camellia nursery.

1937. The yucca lined steps led down the garden to the gate in the boundary wall. This would have been the way guests walked to the beach.

1938. General Sir Bernard Montgomery inspecting Slapton Sands for military landing exercisse, which were carried out in this year, six years prior to 'Exercise Tiger'.

View of the hotel and Slapton sands before 'Exercise Tiger'.

1947. View after the war showing the burnt out shell of the hotel.

Picture of the higher Ley looking up the Gara Valley, near Strete Gate, showing open water and the reeds being harvested for local thatching.

Original watercolour by J.C. Way 1831

1890. The reeds were cut and then placed in the boat before being off loaded onto the shore of the Ley.

The reeds were then stacked in bundles and stood on end to dry out before being used to thatch the roofs in local villages.

The end of another annual holiday for the Chrisford family as they boarded the coach for Dartmouth in front of the fishermen's cottages which stood on the site now occupied by the Venture House. Annie Chrisford can be seen in the window of the carriage holding a baby. About twenty people are being driven to Dartmouth Station by Edward Sanders.

Edward Sanders, first coach driver, 1873

Lewis Guest, last coach driver, 1924

Edward Sanders was born at Virgenstowe between Launceston in Cornwall and Holsworthy in Devon, on February 27th 1850. At some time he must have moved to Above Town, Dartmouth. He died at Torcross on February 6th 1924.

He married Mary Husson at Dodbrooke Church on November 3rd 1874; they had six children, Minnie Ellen, Frank Husson, Alice Muriel, Harry Rickard, Wilfred Edward and Gertrude Mary.

Harry Rickard (my father W. E. S.) was born on October 28th 1882 at Above Town, Dartmouth and died on January 26th 1937 aged 54 years.

He married Rosina Amabel Stone at St. Michael & All Angels Stokenham on January 22nd 1927.

Harry's mother was Mary Husson one of six children, her parents being Edward Husson born 19th February 1819 and Catherine Bowden born November 10th 1818. Catherine was the daughter of John and Ann Bowden.

An extract from *English Coach Drivers* published in 1884 price one shilling.

'The Pioneer and Vivid coaches leave Dartmouth for Kingsbridge via Torcross daily (Sundays excepted). It would take approximately four hours to go from Dartmouth to Kingsbridge at 3s. 6d. single, and 5s. 6d. return. Proprietors – The Dartmouth Coaching Company, Ltd. Manager Mr W. Vickery, Torcross Hotel.'

The history of the above coaches dates back to the year 1873, and the opening scene was laid at the Sands Hotel, Slapton. The principal actor being Mr W. Vickery. This gentleman had taken the Sands Hotel situated about half way between Dartmouth and Kingsbridge, in 1872: he soon discovered that he could not get his daily papers the same day as they were published, and wishing to keep himself informed of what was going on in the world in general, and our tight little island in particular, he conceived the decidedly enterprising idea of running a coach on his own account to fetch his own private letters and daily papers trusting to luck, no doubt, that the coach would soon get known to the travelling public, and fill up. Needless to say, he found it a very loosing game at first, and, to use his own words "he worked it three years at a great loss, especially the first year". However, Mr Vickery was plucky enough to try it a fourth year, with the satisfactory result that he found it beginning to pay; so he secured a partner in the person of Mr Tucker, of Kingsbridge, and together they kept the coach going (and paying) till 1884; when the command for seats had come so great that they started a second coach, and ran both all the year round until 1887. In 1899 Mr Tucker retired from the enterprise, and Mr Vickery worked both coaches on his own account for the next three years, when he turned it into the present company – but retaining the management himself – so popular had the road become that a

third coach, the Comet, was at once put on from Torcross to Dartmouth and back (via Kingsbridge) and has been running daily summer and winter ever since.

E. Sanders, the coachman of the Pioneer, has been with Mr Vickery twenty-one and a half years, has driven 201,880 miles, and carried 110,639 passengers and in that time without an accident. Edward (my Grandfather W. E. S.) managed the coaching company at the Torcross Hotel, until the 1914-1918 war when most of the horses went to the war. This put the end to the coaching company and it finished trading around about 1916.

By this time Edward and his wife were already living at Torcross, in a little cottage now called Little Aish. Some time after the turn of the century he bought a piece of land from Squire Holdsworth and together with his son Harry built the house known as The Elms. Inside the roof on the side wall is marked in the cement 1913, it must have taken several years to complete bearing in mind that all the materials came by horse and cart.

In 1924 Edward Sanders bought a piece of land next to the elms where my father built the garage and petrol station. He paid forty pounds for the land, which he bought from his son Wilfred who had bought the whole field and woods when Frederick John Holdsworth's Widdicombe estate was sold. Wilfred paid five hundred and fifty pounds for the field; he was still in the Air Force stationed Egypt at the time.

Grandfather Edward died on 1st November 1925 his estate was left to his children namely – Minnie Ellen, Alice Muriel, Harry Rickard, Wilfred Edward and Gertrude Mary.

Contributed by Bill Sanders

Harry and Rosina Sanders (Stone)

William and Betsy Stone

Contributed by Bill Sanders

Harry Rickard Sanders born at Above Town, Dartmouth on October 28th 1882. He learnt his trade as a moulder with Simpson, Strickland Co., at the Sandquay shipbuilding yard at Dartmouth. He served six years as an apprentice moulder and worked at the yard until he joined The Royal Engineers as a moulder in the 1914-18 war, he was stationed in France where at some period he was in contact with gas spread by the German army, which in later life affected his health which I think contributed to his early death at the age of 54 years. After the war when he was living with his father at Torcross at The Elms they bought a piece of land next to The Elms for forty pounds from Wilfred Sanders where my father built the garage and petrol station, where he repaired cars, sold petrol and ran a Taxi service.

He married my mother Rosin Amabel Stone at Stokenham Church on January 22nd 1927 and lived at 3 Florence Cottages with my grandfather Stone who mother was looking after, who had had a stroke.

When he first started, before they had the petrol pumps, mother used to help serve the petrol from two-gallon cans and also when they had the pumps. He continued with the garage until he was taken ill and died on January 26th 1937. I was 8 years old when he died; I haven't a good recollection of him, but can remember he used to read me stories lying in bed with a candle on his chest for light to see by, as at this time we did not have electric light in the house. I can remember him driving the taxi.

After he had died mother had to sell the garage and pay off the debts and have the remaining money. With some of this money mother had electricity installed into the house and an outside toilet in place of the old bucket type which used to be emptied, usually Sunday nights, the contents having to be taken over to the allotment and buried, not a nice task. Sometime after this she had a bathroom, toilet and a back kitchen constructed, with hot running water. The cold water came from a well in Hannaford's orchard, but as it was low down in the orchard had to pump the cold water by hand pump to a tank in the roof for the new hot water system, if it was a dry summer the cold water in the well would run low and all the houses in the row would run dry, in this case we had to fetch our water from the tap by the butchers shop which was from the same well, but from a lower outlet in the well.

Bill and May Sanders

John and Sima Sanders (great grandson of Edward)

Richard and Wendy Sanders (great grandson of Edward)

Ronald and Jenny Wakely (nee Sanders – great granddaughter of Edward)

David, Peter, Paul, Donni, Mark (great, great grandchildren of Edward)

Childhood Memories of Stephen Williams, son of Harry and Dorothy

Dartmouth to Kingsbridge by Stage Coach and Four pre 1915

My parents spent their holidays each year at Torcross where my grandfather (G.S. Crisford) had built a large ugly house right on the front. That was in the late 1880s, long before planning permission was necessary. The house is still there and stands out as the monstrosity it is between its less pretentious neighbours. I am glad to say it no longer belongs to any of my family although two branches of the family (Grahamsmiths and Venmores) still live in Torcross.

In the days when I knew it well the main road to Torcross ran right along the sea-front in a straight line past the Royal Sands Hotel at Slapton to the Torcross Hotel where it turned sharp right and continued (as it does today) skirting the Ley in the direction of Stokenham and Kingsbridge. (The site of the Royal Sands Hotel which was blown-up in the second world war is marked by a monument on the beach about three-quarters of a mile on the Dartmouth side of Torcross).

Since my immediate family lived in London, where my father was an Anglican Priest in East London, our holiday trips to Torcross were made by train to Kingswear, by ferryboat to Dartmouth and by stage-coach to Torcross. To get the family to Paddington Station my father hired one of the Great Western's small railway buses (horse-drawn of course), which the Railway Companies then provided to transport families to and from their main-line stations. The cost was only a matter of a few shillings and a shilling in those days (5p now) was enough to pay the postage stamps for twelve letters. The railway bus was also far less bother than struggling to travel by public transport with parents, three and later four children and all their luggage – and of course in the early decades of the twentieth century very few ordinary families had motor-cars.

On the train we always had a 'Reserved Compartment' costing five shillings extra on top of the price of the second-class rail tickets for the journey. (There were First, Second and Third Class carriages on the train in those days). My parents always took along a picnic lunch and tea to eat on the train which helped to pass the five hours or so which were pretty dull until the first sight of the sea (around Dawlish) made the trip a bit more interesting for us youngsters.

At Kingswear there always seemed to be plenty of railway-porters around to collect the family luggage from the train and trundle it along on a four-wheeled trolley, which bounced noisily over the wooden flooring as it was pulled through the long bridge-like corridor from the platforms to the landing stage where the ferryboat Mew awaited us. My first Mew, of which I remember very little, was I think a fairly ordinary-looking craft with no obvious bow or stern. It was impossible to tell in which direction she would travel until she actually got going, for from above she must have looked in shape rather like a rugger ball with rounder than usual ends to the oval. This shape of Mew was maintained for a good many years and I seem to remember it still operating just before the 1939-45 war.

From the ferry when it arrived at Dartmouth the passengers walked up the slope giving up their railway tickets on the way, for Dartmouth Station was listed as a station and really looked like a railway-station although it was the only railway-station in Britain which had no railway lines and had never seen a train closer than from across the river. All the tickets issued there were railway-tickets printed for journeys from Dartmouth and the tickets covering the journey from elsewhere were issued to Dartmouth.

Outside Dartmouth Station one of the Dartmouth-Kingsbridge stagecoaches with four horses would be waiting. The luggage was loaded from the railway trolley into the coach's boot. The passengers, if elderly or if the weather was very bad, took seats inside the body of the coach while the younger or more agile climbed on the top. I being a bit spoiled perhaps was invariably settled beside the coachman on his box. On the back of the coach there rode the guard with his horn, which he blew at blind corners and to warn the villages en route that the coach was arriving. I don't remember much about the guards; to me they were never as glamorous as the coachmen.

Two stagecoaches maintained the Dartmouth-Kingsbridge service, a brown (or yellowish) one and a black one. Coachman Sanders drove the brown coach and Coachman Guest (who, my boyhood memory recalls had a very big nose) drove the black coach. Sanders was my favourite – he actually let me drive the four-in-hand, or I thought he did although of course he was only pretending and always kept the vital parts of the reins firmly in his own hands, but it made me feel very grand!

When the coach had to go downhill there were heavy iron shoes, which had to be pushed under the rear wheels. The guard had the job of doing this and in the case of lesser gradients he would walk behind the coach controlling the hand brakes which had to be wound on and off by a wheel at the back of the boot. There were two major hills on the Dartmouth-Torcross section of the route. One was a three-mile hill between Dartmouth and Stoke Fleming and the other was a much steeper hill with a nasty right angle bend before the long straight Line to Torcross.

On the trip towards Torcross once the coach was safely down at sea-level the horses could almost gallop, but not quite, along the Line until they came to the tall structure on the seaward side of the road just before the first building in the Torcross village. This erection was a life-saving rocket launcher to help in the case of ships in distress in Start Bay. I never saw it in operation.

From the rocket house the horses took the coach road along the front at a moderate trot, which gave the coachman the chance to toss letters, newspapers and small packets to the various cottages towards their front doors. I always regarded this as Coachman Sanders' speciality but I have no doubt Coachman Guest did the same thing.

The coach-stop at Torcross was outside the Torcross Hotel and here there was often a change of horses. Their stables were (and I believe the building is still there) at the rear of the hotel a few yards up the little hill, which runs up alongside the hotel. It was always a great boyhood thrill to watch the old team being unharnessed, the leaders from the front end of the coach-shaft, then the leaders, already harnessed to their draw-bar which a stableman carried behind them and finally hooked onto the front of the coach shaft. The reins were buckled up, the coachman climbed onto the 'box', the guard blew his horn and the coach-and-four moved off.

The last time I rode on the Dartmouth-Kingsbridge stagecoach was during the First World War when I was six years old. Soon the coaches were withdrawn and replaced by hideous unromantic motor charabancs marked GWR. I thought them so horrible that unconsciously I must have 'switched-off' my memory for I recall hardly any thing about them. Very sadly, though, I did hear that the two coaches were auctioned and fetched just £2 each – for their wheels – their bodywork then being of no interest or practical use to anyone.

Stephen Williams (brother to Betty) – June 1991

Lewis Guest and Emma (nee Gillard) – Ethel, Frederick, Alfred (Beatrice not yet born).

Lewis Guest was born in Loddiswell and married for the first time when he was very young, at the age of 17. He had four children, the youngest being Beatrice (Triff). Always generous and fond of children he later adopted Harold Stevens when Harold's mother (a seasonal worked at the Greyhomes Hotel) could no longer afford to keep her own baby. Harold was then brought up as one of his own.

Lewis was employed by the Dartmouth Coaching Company and for many years he drove one of their horse-drawn carriages between Kingsbridge and Dartmouth. He had the honour of driving the last ever coach to leave Dartmouth Station in 1924 (see photos on the coach road between Kingsbridge and Dartmouth).

He then set up in business on his own as a 'Carrier of Goods' with his own horse and cart. He kept his horse in the stable between the butchers and Florence Cottages where he lived. He would collect parcels, etc. from Kingsbridge station then pick up any goods from the shops in Fore Street to be delivered along the main road from Kingsbridge to Torcross. He was always very popular with the local children as he used to let them ride along on top of his cart in exchange for them doing the legwork when the parcel or goods needed to be taken up to the front door of the recipient. He finally hung up his reins and retired in 1938.

When his first wife died he remarried, this time to Miss Avis Prettyjohn. They had no further children, but he continued to enjoy the company of other villagers and their families by taking them out in his boat whenever he went fishing.

Taffy and Triff Sutton (nee Beatrice Guest).

Beatrice (Triff) Guest married Taffy Sutton who was born in South Wales, but came to live in Kingsbridge when his mother died. They were married in 1927 and came to live in Torcross at Myrtle Cottage. During the evacuations they moved to Churchstow.
They had three children David, Michael and Anne.

Ray and Anne Pengelly (nee Sutton).

Anne Sutton met Ray Pengelly (the son of a local thatcher and mole catcher) at one of the many village hall dances that they both used to frequent. They were married in 1962 and lived with Taffy and Triff while they built their own house in the field behind Myrtle Cottage where they brought up their three children Andrew, Sandra and Stuart. Sandra still lives in Torcross with her three boys Samuel, Luke and Isaac.

*Andrew, Stuart and Sandra Pengelly
(great grandchildren of Lewis Guest).*

*Luke, Isaac and Samuel (great, great
grandchildren of Lewis Guest).*

Four Generations of Hannafords the Butcher

John 1st Generation butcher with sons Reg (died age 17) and Edward.

Mr John Hannaford came to Torcross in 1897 and took over the business from Mrs Lidstone and her son. They were tenants of the Widdicombe Estate. They also rented some fields behind the shop where they had the slaughterhouse, and kept chickens, (for eggs as well as meat) ducks and geese. They also kept cows and had a milk round in the village until 1934. When Widdicombe Estate was broken up they bought the shop, Prideaux House, and some fields for the sum of £1300. John Edward joined his father after World War One. (He was the father of John, Reg, George, Margaret and Una). They kept a horse and cart to make deliveries as far as Frogmore and then through to Prawle including Hallsand and Beesands. (There were already two butchers in Slapton).

Keeping the meat fresh was a constant problem in the shop; ice was brought from the fish industry in Brixham and delivered by carrier from Dartmouth, and kept in a zinc icebox. When electricity came to the village in 1935 they bought a cold room, which is still the one used in the shop although it has had to have a few new motors over the years. There was no cooling in the delivery vehicles and in summer they would hang a large bunch of mint in the wagon to distract the customers' noses. At the beginning of the week they would have beef and lamb to sell and at the end beef and pork. Meat that had not sold on the round was brined and many people lived on it, rarely fresh meat. They made two hundred weight of sausages a week, which were much more peppery than today, partly in case they were a bit 'pindy'. They would buy the meat direct from the farmers and slaughter it in Torcross. Pigs were butchered in the washhouse because they could heat up the water essential for pig butchery. The copper was tended by the copper man.

John died in 1960, but John, Reg and George had been working in the business since the end of rationing in 1954. The business went on much the same except for the changes in their customers' tastes. When the weather was bad, they would go to their customers through rain, gales and snow, and once when the Line was closed Reg went round via Dartmouth road to Slapton, and in the snow out to Prawle including a walk down to Maelcombe House with their order. The grateful customers thought a 'tot' would warm them up!

George left the business in 1994 taking the slaughterhouse with him. At this point there were changes as the animals were killed elsewhere and the tradition of using all parts of the animal was no longer allowed. The paunches and tripes had gone to feed local kennels and the hunt dogs, the intestines had gone to the fell-mongers for sausage skins, or perhaps tennis racquet strings, and the hides were cured and sent to Spain to make leather goods.

By this time John's son, John the fourth, was working in the shop, and was joined by his brother Richard when John senior and Reg retired after working there through the centenary of the business in 1997. They are still there carrying on the fine tradition.

The experience that Reg gained from buying livestock from the farmers for the shop was so respected that he was asked to judge at various local shows including Kingsbridge and Totnes and the Christmas show at Tavistock. He was invited and has judged the Devon County Show four times.

There cannot be many villages the size of Torcross that have their own butcher, and indeed if they had not been able to sell so much from the delivery vans in the surrounding area no doubt it would not have been viable. There certainly are not many butchers where the queue forms down the garden, and gaze out down the Ley while waiting to be served!

Edward and Chris Hannaford, second generation, Reg, Margaret, John, Una and George.

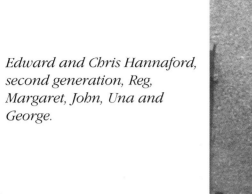

Beatrice Pike with baby Una, Margaret, Reg, John and George.

Reg, George and John on farmer Baker's horse (milkman).

John, Reg, George, third Generation butchers.

The Hannafords with husbands and wives.

John and Richard, the present generation butchers.

Nigel, Maureen, Reg Hannaford.

Great grandchildren of Edward – (Reg's) Victoria and James.

Grand children of Edward – Catherine, Richard, Deborah, Susan, John.

Great grandchildren of Edward, John, Simon, Tom, Andrew, Peter, Clare, Karen and Melissa.

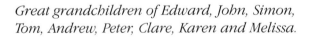

The Simmons Family

The Walter-Symons Family (from Coleridge Farm, Chillington).
The young man second from the right, back row is Thomas (husband of Alice).

Alice Walter-Symons (wife of Thomas) – Mildred Simmons (nee Walter-Symons).

Jimmy Simmons

Angie Lansdale (nee Simmons).

Barry, Sophie, Michael, Alec and William.

The Chrisford family (one of the original second home owners), 1880

George Chrisford

Annie Chrisford

Rev. Harry and Dorothy Williams (nee Chrisford).

William and Betty Venmore (nee Williams), John, Ruth, Chris and Marjorie.

The Kellond Family

1881. George and Hannah Kellond.

1923. Bill Kellond (with the waist-coat, in front of the threshing machine).

1920 Peter Kellond (Coalman).

Peter Kellond, Horace Stone, Brian Stone.

Brian Stone

166

The Rogers Family

Denis and Mary Rogers owned the Torcross Hotel between 1947 and 1981.

The Rogers Family – Sheena, Edward Noyce, Alison, Robin Rose-Price, Mary, Denis and Martin.

2001. Alison Rose-Price (nee Rogers).   Robin Rose-Price

1998. Sarah and Andrew Rose-Price.

The Garner Family

First generation, Robert Garner.

Second generation, Joan and Peter Garner with eldest daughter Gillian.

Third generation, Sheena and Howard Garner with their children Isabel and William.

169

Other Torcross Residents

Harold and Jane Stevens in 'Harold's Field' (in front of Greyhomes Hotel).

Bill and Anne Dunlop.

Ralph Hannaford Blank
Aged 21
Born 17th September, 1893

Arthur William Blank
Aged 19
Born 14th October, 1895

Sons of Thomas Chadder Blank and Anne Hannaford, late of Thrift Cottage, Torcross
   Thomas Chadder Blank, mariner of Stokenham, born 12th August, 1851, married Anne Hannaford of Slapton (born 1855?) on 15th December, 1874.
   Thomas Chadder Blank, along with his 11-year-old son, John Henry (born 4th November, 1883) were drowned in Start Bay on 12th July,1895. They are buried together in Stokenham churchyard overlooking the sea.

Anne Blank

1895. Stokenham School.

1938. Stokenham School.

1947. Stokenbam School

1953. Coronation

1951. Angela Simmons' party at the Torcross Hotel.

1951. Jimmy Simmons' party at the Torcross Hotel.

1955. Sunday School at Stokenham Church.

1954. Sunday School Nativity Play organised by Mrs Gibbons.